JOURNEY INTO SILENCE

TRANSFORMATION THROUGH CONTEMPLATION, WONDER, AND WORSHIP

JOURNEY INTO
SILENCE

TRANSFORMATION THROUGH
CONTEMPLATION, WONDER, AND WORSHIP

AUTHOR OF *HEBREW WORD STUDY*
CHAIM BENTORAH

WHITAKER
HOUSE

JOURNEY INTO SILENCE:
Transformation Through Contemplation, Wonder, and Worship

Chaim Bentorah
www.chaimbentorah.com
chaimbentorah@gmail.com

ISBN: 978-1-62911-912-0
eBook ISBN: 978-1-62911-913-7
Printed in the United States of America
© 2018 by Chaim Bentorah

Whitaker House
1030 Hunt Valley Circle
New Kensington, PA 15068
www.whitakerhouse.com

Library of Congress Cataloging-in-Publication Data
LC record available at https://lccn.loc.gov/2017053483.

1 2 3 4 5 6 7 8 9 10 11 ᴑ 25 24 23 22 21 20 19 18

"Be still, and know that I am God."
—Psalm 46:10

CONTENTS

PREFACE

ENTERING A WORLD OF CONTEMPLATION, WONDER, AND WORSHIP

Many years ago, when I was teaching Hebrew at World Harvest Bible College, I met a Catholic priest who was passing through South Bend, Indiana, to attend a retreat sponsored by Notre Dame University. As a good evangelical Christian, I asked who the retreat speakers would be and what workshops were planned. He looked at me rather confused and said, "This is a silent retreat." He went on to explain that he was going to stay in a cabin in the woods and spend one full week living in complete solitude, having no interaction with anyone except God and His creation. He would focus on communing with God as he fasted, prayed, and studied the Bible. For seven days, 24/7, he would be alone with the Lord in silence.

The priest's comments fascinated me because I had previously heard many rabbis talk about the beauty of silence. In fact, one rabbi told me that in silence, you can hear the world weep. The rabbis had indicated that when we take time to be quiet, we connect with God and with people who are hurting in a way we would never do otherwise.

Through these contacts, the concept of taking a silent retreat myself began to form in my mind. Another major thread contributing to my interest in silent retreats came from my study of the Scriptures, where I found that many of the great men of God, such as Moses, Elijah, David, John the Baptist, and Jesus Himself, spent time in solitude, communing with the Lord and receiving spiritual strength. Although silence is practiced in various forms, and is applied by people of different world religions, it is deeply rooted in the Bible. But while I saw the exercise of solitude incorporated within Judaism and Catholicism, I found no real avenues within my own Protestant evangelical world for those who wished to spend some time in silence in order to devote themselves to listening to God, learning from Him, and growing spiritually.

In Protestant Christianity, we do hold various types of retreats, but these are normally filled with speakers and fellowship, and silence is not often encouraged. Similarly, our conferences and conventions are usually crowded and noisy, with little opportunity for attendees to go off alone and meditate on God and the Scriptures. Yet C. S. Lewis expressed that one of the devil's greatest tools is noise—he hates silence, because in silence you start to think, and when you think, God begins to reveal Himself to you.

Still, I think the longing for silence seems to be embedded in us as Christians, because I do find little hints of it within evangelical churches, even though it is somewhat downplayed. We call it "getting ourselves in the mood for worship," "moments of meditation," or "having our morning quiet time." I have even experienced a movement called "soaking." I visited a Canadian church where soaking had its origins, and I found people lying on the floor with their eyes closed, some quietly praying, some with uplifted hands, and some apparently sleeping or caught up in the spiritual realm. Each one seemed to be longing for intimacy with God and seeking silence before Him.

I think all believers in Jesus Christ who have a relationship with a personal God will sense a yearning to spend uninterrupted time with the Lord—to get to know Him, to experience His presence, and to see His glory. Regardless of whether we attend a denominational or nondenominational church, we have a hunger for deep fellowship with Him.

And that is how it was—and is—for me. For many years after I began to note the practice of solitude in the Bible and encountered the Catholic priest en route to his silent retreat, the idea of spending extended time in silence kept coming back to me and filling my thoughts, until I realized God was calling me to do the same thing. I searched the Internet and found the Abbey of Gethsemani, a monastery outside Louisville, Kentucky, that was open to hosting individuals for weeklong silent retreats. I contacted them, and even though I was not Catholic, they welcomed me to come and stay for a retreat of silence among the Trappist monks who devote themselves to solitude and contemplative prayer. It was a transformational experience.

The following year, I rented a small cabin in the Catskill Mountains of New York and spent a week in silence again. The third year, I felt the call of God to return to the abbey for another week of solitude. And I plan to continue to go on silent retreats every year.

My journeys to the Abbey of Gethsemani and to the Catskills were deliberate acts of setting aside focused time to seek God. I was putting myself in a situation where I would have no distractions, nothing else to demand my attention, for an extended period of time. Like Moses, I sought only the glory of God so I could know Him better. (See Exodus 33:18.)

Living in silence tends to mimic fasting. By the third day, the supernatural is apt to become more natural than the natural. God becomes so real during a time of solitude that you weep out of pure joy as you are caught up in His presence. The depths of God's heart of compassion open up to you as never before. It becomes both a spiritual and an emotional journey that brings healing, release, and renewed ministry to others.

Throughout my silent retreats, I kept journals of my ongoing journey into silence. Writing a journal is my way of meditation. In keeping with my daily practice, I wrote Hebrew word study devotionals of the Scripture passages that God led me to. As a Hebrew teacher with a knowledge of ancient languages and Jewish literature, I was able to peer into the very depths of the words I studied. As my journey into silence progressed, so did the reach of my understanding of each word.

After I returned from these retreats, whenever I shared my experiences with others, it seemed as if a light would click on inside them, and you could tell they were thinking something such as, *What would it be like to spend one week in an environment where I did nothing but live a contemplative life with no contact with the outside world? Just me and God, with nothing to distract me?* They had never before considered such a thing. From time to time, they might have participated in the discipline of spending up to a full week in fasting, but the idea of withdrawing from the world for a week of silent communion with God was remote to them.

It was because of the interest people expressed, as well as the lack of emphasis on solitude I have seen in the evangelical community, that I decided to adapt the journals from my first three silent retreats into one book with a devotional format, hoping that others would see how silence could enable them to experience the presence of God in a new way. I do not include the entirety of my journals here, because many of the things I experienced are too personal and are meant for my heart and God's alone. However, I have included those portions that I feel open and led to share.

I want to emphasize that you don't have to be a super-spiritual saint to go on a silent retreat. Even though I am a Hebrew teacher, I am an "average Joe," no different from most people. I have no great or exciting testimony of having had a dramatic healing or a deliverance from addiction, or of being saved out of a life of crime and prison. I grew up in a Christian home, with godly parents who raised me to know and love Jesus. I merely hungered and thirsted for God and drank of His living waters, which made me even hungrier and thirstier for more.

I now invite you to join me on this *Journey into Silence*, where we will primarily interact only with God and His creation. Let me share with you some of the amazing and joyful experiences of what it is like to have your mind stayed on Jesus 24/7. Perhaps you, too, will be encouraged to enter this silent world of contemplation, wonder, and worship.

AUTHOR'S NOTE

A UNIQUE APPROACH TO SILENT RETREATS

I have discovered that people go on silent retreats for various reasons. They may be looking for direction and guidance for their lives. They may want to work through pain or grief. They may be seeking rest and peace after a turbulent period of life. They may simply want to draw closer to God.

I have received many spiritual and emotional benefits while seeking the heart of God in silence. However, I approached my silent retreats in a somewhat different way from most who take such journeys, due to my particular background, and this has had a strong influence on the reflections in these pages. I have spent forty years studying various ancient languages, including Hebrew, Greek, and Aramaic, along with the teachings of Jewish sages and rabbis. As a result, this book is distinct not only because it depicts the uncommon practice of living in solitude, but also because it examines the deeper meanings of words and phrases in the Scriptures in light of my experiences with God in silence.

For those who have not previously read my Hebrew Word Study books or blog, I write daily devotional studies in which I incorporate my background in ancient languages and cultures with my personal experiences in an endeavor to find the best English translations for Hebrew words in select scriptural passages. I take this approach because Biblical, or Classical, Hebrew has only seventy-five hundred words, compared with Modern Hebrew, which has a quarter of a million words. Since the ancient language is very nuanced, each word of Classical Hebrew can have multiple meanings. Much of the Bible translation process involves a close examination of the context, the culture of the day, and the idioms in order to determine which of the many possible English words to apply to a given Hebrew word in a specific verse. Additionally, I have learned from Jewish rabbis that we must put a Hebrew word into its emotional context. Hebrew is an emotional language, a language of poets, and thus there is an emotional context involved in many passages of Scripture. I was even taught through rabbinic literature how to interpret and translate words letter by letter. You will find that I employ these rabbinic approaches in the word studies included in this book.

As with other Semitic languages, the original Hebrew alphabet is consonantal, with no separate letters for vowels. Nevertheless, vowel sounds were used in the Hebrew language, because it is impossible to pronounce a word without using the sounds represented by *a, e, i, o,* and *u.* In rabbinic Hebrew, the letters aleph, hei, yod, and vav can be used to denote a vowel. However, the proper pronunciation of Classical Hebrew was lost about twenty-five hundred years ago when it became a "dead" language and was no longer spoken. Around the seventh century AD, the Masoretic text introduced the *niqqud,* which are a series of dots and dashes placed near a consonantal letter to indicate a vowel. (This is not considered part of the inspired text.) The normal pattern is: consonant, vowel, consonant, vowel.

Even though many people who learn Hebrew words like to speak the terms aloud, pronouncing a particular word adds little to no value to the process of seeking to arrive at an appropriate rendering of its meaning; thus, in this book, I have not placed any emphasis on the actual pronunciation of the words. My main concern is to drill down to the very core of a Hebrew word using its trilateral, or three-consonant, root. I use the *abajab,* or the consonantal alphabet, and follow a rabbinic tradition of defaulting to using the letter *a* whenever any vowel is needed, except in cases where I explain a certain word usage or grammatical expression. Occasionally, when I feel it is necessary, I will use the Masoretic text's version of the vowels. Furthermore, while many academic texts use left-handed apostrophes for the letter aleph and right-handed apostrophes for the letter ayin, I have streamlined the practice for this book, using right-handed apostrophes for both.

In all my word studies, my goal is to explore the secondary and optional meanings of biblical words in order to better understand them, to seek the origins of terms, and to plug them into the context of verses or passages to see if they fit, and if so, if they might provide a deeper spiritual message to apply to our lives. Please note that I offer these reflections on Scripture not as an academic exercise or to propose a separate Bible translation but solely as a devotional tool. The ultimate purpose is to open up the depths of God's Word in order to draw us into an intimate relationship with the Lord, while at the same time refreshing and challenging us in our spiritual lives. Thus, the silent retreats that I describe in *Journey into Silence* have been an extension of my ongoing desire to seek the compassionate heart of God through His multifaceted, inspired Word.

PART ONE
CALLED TO SILENCE

PROLOGUE: THE SILENT SPEAKING OF GOD

"I looked and there was a whirlwind coming from the north, a
great cloud with fire flashing back and forth and brilliant light all
around it. In the center of the fire, there was a gleam like amber."
—Ezekiel 1:4 (HCSB)

Is the idea of listening to God in silence a new concept for you? Before we
begin part one of *Journey into Silence*, let's explore a fascinating Hebrew
term and what I believe it teaches us about our opportunity to listen to
God with our hearts and hear what He wants to speak to us.

In the above verse, the Hebrew term that the prophet Ezekiel used for
the concept translated *"a gleam like amber"* is *chashmal*. This word is used
only three times in the Old Testament—all in Ezekiel (1:4, 27; and 8:2),
all in the same context, and all describing what Ezekiel saw as the center of
the manifestation of God Himself.

Scholars consider the word *chasmal* to be of unknown origin. That is,
they don't know the root word from which it was derived. Since we don't
really know what the root word of *chashmal* is, we have to do the best we
can at interpreting what the term signifies. Most scholars believe *chashmal*
refers to a bright shining object. The majority of translators simply follow
tradition and render the word as either a shining or gleaming amber or
metal. But let's explore some other ideas.

The Septuagint, a Koine Greek translation of the Old Testament, uses
the word *elektron* when translating *chashmal*. Interestingly, *elektron* is the
word from which our terms *electric* and *electricity* are derived. Perhaps in

his vision, Ezekiel saw God manifested in the form of lightning, especially as Ezekiel 1:4 includes this description: *"fire flashing back and forth and brilliant light all around it."*

Chashmal has also been translated as *electrum*, a Latin term derived from *elektron. Electrum* is a naturally occurring alloy of gold and silver, whose colors range from pale yellow to bright yellow like the sun. In ancient times, it was a precious metal used in coinage. Today, it is used as an excellent conductor of electricity. The Hebrews considered gold to represent the light or glory of God, and silver to represent His holiness. The two are combined in one element in *electrum*.

Furthermore, the Talmud teaches that *chashmal* might be a compound word meaning "silence" (*chash*) and "speaking" (*milel*). This makes me think of how electricity is silent, yet "speaks" to us in its flashes. (Thunder is only the *effect* of lightning on the air in its path, not its "voice.") Perhaps the sages recognized the energy in lightning and felt it was a silent witness of God.

For myself, I agree with the Talmud's interpretation. I have come to believe that the *chashmal* of God refers to silence and speaking in silence, so that what Ezekiel saw in the center of the fire was *the silent speaking of God*. And that is what we seek in times of solitude with God—we seek all that He desires to communicate to us in His silent speaking.

How can we learn to hear this silent speaking? I read something very interesting in the Talmud in Chagiga 13b regarding the mystery of prayer: "For one to connect to the *chashmal* of God, one first must be silent to cut away the *kelipos*. One then can hear the *milel* [speaking] of God." We must be silent before we can perceive God's silent speaking, because our silence cuts away the *kelipos* that hinders us from hearing Him.

Kelipos literally means "a shell," and as Rabbi Yaacov Yosef characterized, *kelipos* are fleshly thoughts that come during prayer. How often our prayers are filled with fleshly thoughts so that we cannot hear God. In my most recent silent retreat, it took me almost three days before I started to really pray. Up until that time, my prayers were filled with *kelipos*, fleshly thoughts and desires. But after a period of silence, after a time of joining with creation in worship of the Creator, I began to pray prayers that were not filled with fleshly desires, but only spiritual ones. I grew hungry for the

Word of God, and I would stay up late at night continuing to read God's Word, which was burning away all the *kelipos* in my mind and heart.

When silence before God cracks the shell of our fleshly thoughts, it ushers in the presence or pleasure of God—and when we are in His presence, He speaks to us in silence. During all of my silent retreats, I have heard the cry of the world; I have heard the world weep in sorrow and despair. I believe this was the *chashmal*, or silent speaking, of God, sharing with me the burdens of His heart for this lost world.

There are perhaps many Christians who have not yet entered into true prayer, or *chashmal*. If you find it difficult to pray, perhaps you just need to sit in silence for a while—maybe for a long while. During that time, think about God, fill your mind with His Word, meditate on His attributes, and before long you will break through the *kelipos* and enter into authentic prayer. And you will hear God speaking in silence.

When you break through, you will be amazed at how easy it is to hear Him, and how you can spend hours in prayer without even realizing it. In fact, you will grow to desire the *chashmal* of God more than food and sleep. I know—I have experienced this, just as I believe Ezekiel did and attempted to describe. Until you experience that *chashmal*, Ezekiel's vision may mean nothing more to you than an abstract description of a lightning storm. But if you experience the *chashmal* of God, this vision will be a beautiful depiction of the love and passion of God, who speaks to us powerfully in His silence.

1

REST

*"Thus saith the LORD, The heaven is my throne,
and the earth is my footstool: where is the house that ye build unto
me? and where is the place of my rest?"*
—Isaiah 66:1

It is my first day in silence at the Abbey of Gethsemani, and I am sitting outside the chapel overlooking a beautiful pasture and watching a mourning dove flutter across the ground. I just opened my Hebrew Bible and pointed my finger to the first verse I came to. We are usually warned against this practice of Bible reading as being too random or "mystic" to be trustworthy, and I agree that we should recognize its hazards. Believe me, I know the joke about the old boy who felt he needed a word from the Lord, so he closed his eyes, opened his Bible, and blindly let his finger fall on the page, so that it just happened to rest on the verse that says, *"And [Judas] went and hanged himself"* (Matthew 27:5). Not happy with that result, the man tried again, and this time his finger fell on the verse that says, *"Go, and do thou likewise"* (Luke 10:37)!

But haven't most Christians, at one time or another, used this "method" of opening up the Bible to a seemingly random verse, only to find genuine comfort or insight from God? I think that if we are discerning about it, we can sometimes recognize Him speaking to us in this way. So now, as I begin my time of solitude, I have opened to Isaiah 66:1, noting especially the last part of the verse, where God asks, *"Where is the place of my rest?"*

The Hebrew word translated *"rest"* in this verse is *manuchah*, which means quiet or silent. It comes from the root word *nuchah*, meaning a peaceful abode or a place of quietness. It is a restful environment absent of discord. I haven't considered the context of this verse yet, but I sense God is trying to start me off on the right foot. I need to find His silent or quiet place—His place for resting in silence.

I recognize that even my search for silence has become a selfish thing: *my* seeking, *my* longings, *my* desires. Yet what is it that God desires? And why would He seek silence? I think more about this phrase, *"Where is the place of my rest?"* Perhaps God has called me to silence because He wants to spend some time resting in the silence with me. Perhaps He is seeking to commune with me without my mind being distracted by my daily activities or sidetracked by *"the cares of this world"* (Mark 4:19)—to just sit down and chat together in an atmosphere of peace and calm. Times of tension in our lives are not the best time for God to talk over serious matters with us about our future or about major decisions. Those discussions are best held during moments of *nuchah*.

(I've begun to realize that if I receive revelation from God during this silent retreat, there will be no one I can immediately share it with. I cannot access my e-mail, and although I am not required to remain at the abbey and can leave the compound at any time, to do so would seem to violate God's call upon me to spend a week with Him here in solitude. As a teacher, this is hard for me, because I love to share knowledge and insights about the Bible. But I accept the fact that, at least for the present, if I get a revelation or an insight, it is for me, and me alone.)

Checking into this verse further, I find that the word translated *"where"* comes from two words in the original Hebrew, *'ay zeh*, which are used as a single unit. Together, these words have various meanings, such as "where," "what," "why," "how," "when," "behold," and "who." Judging from the context, including the following verse, it appears that a proper rendering would be, "Who is my silence?" or rather, "Who is the one I can find in silence or stillness?" The answer is found in Isaiah 66:2: *"But to this man will I look, even to him that is poor and of a contrite spirit, and trembleth at my word."*

The Hebrew word translated *"poor"* is *'ane*, which indicates someone who is depressed in mind or circumstances. Indeed, my personal circumstances are very depressing to me right now. It is also the person who has a *"contrite spirit."* The word *"contrite"* in Hebrew is *nakah*, which means dejected. I claim that part of the verse for myself also. Third, it is someone who has a reverence for God's Word, which would apply to me as well.

So I come to this place of silence in the midst of my depressed circumstances and dejected spirit. How can this be the place where God will find His rest? I think I understand. I had barely begun this retreat of silence before I began to weep. The Hebrew word for "weep" is *baki*, and the word for "heart" is *lev*. Both of these words have the same numerical value in Hebrew, and the Jewish sages teach that this emphasizes that weeping comes from the heart. My heart weeps because I know that my pride, my unclean thoughts, and my attitudes have wounded God's heart. Yet by giving my heart room to weep, I also allow God the opportunity to reach into my heart and forgive the wounds I have brought to His heart. And it is in that place that He finds His rest, because He is once more restored to fellowship with one whom He loves.

⌁

While I was enjoying my first meal at the abbey today, someone broke the rule of silence. He spoke quietly, and only to ask a brother a question. However, in the silence of the room, it was like a booming voice, and all heads turned toward the sound. Interestingly, I had just read Isaiah 66:6, which can be translated, "Hark, an uproar from the city." The Hebrew word for "uproar" is *sha'on*, which is a crashing sound, like a wave hitting the rocks on a shore. In the context of this verse, the uproar is a noise from the temple, a sound that does not belong there. It is as if the Lord is reminding me that for this week of silence, I must beware of any "uproar," or *sha'on*—anything that does not belong in this retreat of silence. I must not let the voice of my health concerns, my ministry concerns, my financial concerns, or any other voice intrude on this time that God and I have together. This is *His* time, not my health concern time, my ministry concern time, or my financial concern time. God cannot find His rest in me—or I in Him—if these voices intrude.

Although I have already wept through my repentance, I still weep. I know now it is not I who weep but God who is weeping in me as I join my heart with His. I feel His pain and sorrow for those who have broken His heart. But God's heart also weeps for the pain and suffering of this world. To be honest, I fear that I have not risen to this level of weeping. Perhaps, during this time of silence, I will rise to that level. Perhaps, in silence, I will hear the cry of this world with the ears of my heart, I will see the suffering of this world with the eyes of my heart, and maybe, maybe, God will allow me to speak to the suffering with the lips of my heart. Dear precious Father God, my dearest Friend, Companion, and Counselor, please let it be so.

2

CORRECTION

"Come now, and let us reason together, saith the LORD:
though your sins be as scarlet, they shall be as white as snow;
though they be red like crimson, they shall be as wool."
—Isaiah 1:18

What a strange environment I am in at this silent retreat. You have no social obligations or duties. There is no phone, no Internet—actually, no communication with others whatsoever. You are not required to attend mass or daily prayers, or join the brothers in their chants, if you do not desire. No one is watching you, no one says "hi" or even acknowledges your presence. When your time is up, you simply drop your key in a little box and leave. There is no one to say goodbye to, nor any bill to settle up. There is only one Person you are here to speak with; there is only one Friend to make or renew a friendship with.

It is now three o'clock in the afternoon, and I am sitting in a garden. For just a moment, I am tempted to look for a schedule to find out who the speaker is tonight or what workshops are available. But, of course, there are no speakers or workshop leaders. I have attended many conferences and been on many retreats; I have heard some of the best speakers, teachers, and preachers at these events, but this is the first retreat where God Himself is the Keynote (and only) Speaker and Workshop Leader—and He is speaking 24/7.

Well, perhaps there is a guest speaker after all. A bird has just flown to a tree right in front of me. He is looking directly at me now and chirping.

Suddenly, he flies right toward me. I duck, but he passes by me. It was as if he wanted to make sure he had my attention. I look back at the tree where he had been perched. It is a massive tree, and, unlike all the other trees around, it appears to be pure white, including its bark. At first, I think that the tree is dead, but then I notice it has very light-colored, green leaves. The "guest speaker" was a blackbird, and although the tree is huge, I could not help but see that little black speck against those pale leaves.

I feel drawn to read Isaiah 1:18: *"Come now, and let us reason together."* The Hebrew word translated *"reason together"* is *yakach,* which means to correct, to bring into right order, to bring into harmony, or to be in tune. The blackbird was not in harmony with that tree; he was totally out of tune with it because the tree was an entirely different color than he was. A white dove would be in harmony with that white tree. Perhaps the message is that I am out of harmony with the purity of God?

In Isaiah 1:18, God is saying, in effect, "Come, let us get corrected in our relationship." The Hebrew verb for "get corrected" is in a cohortative form, which indicates exhortation. God is asking me to join Him in a correcting process whereby I can be in harmony with Him. I think again about the blackbird. His feathers could never permanently change color to become like a dove's. No, the only way he could be a dove would be if he were born a dove. To change, he would have to be born again.

"Lord, I renew that prayer I made fifty years ago to be born again. Come, let us be united together and make a correction in my life. Though my sins be as scarlet, make them as white as snow, like this tree made of the same type of material as the cross upon which You died."

God will take all my sins, mistakes, and failures, and make them as white as snow. The Hebrew word for *"snow"* in this verse is *shalag. Shalag* begins with the Hebrew letter shin, which signifies God's passionate love. God will take all my sins and cover them with His passionate love. The next letter is lamed, which indicates teaching. He will teach me and instruct me in the way represented by the final letter, gimmel, which signifies His loving-kindness.

Apparently as a confirmation from God about my meditations, one of the retreat members just walked past my white tree. He is dressed all in white—he even has white hair—so that he blended right in with the white tree. I feel God is affirming that because of the sacrifice of Jesus on the Tree two thousand years ago, my heart truly is as white as snow and in harmony with His.

3

PURGING AWAY THE DROSS

"I will…purge away thy dross as with lye,
and will take away all thine alloy."
—Isaiah 1:25 (JPS Tanakh 1917)

I checked out the abbey's library, although I didn't find much variety among the books. But then, this is a monastery and not a university. There seemed to be a lot of books on grief and dealing with illnesses, tragedies, and life's many stresses. I had never stopped to consider this before, but while I've observed a number of priests who have come to the abbey for the purpose of refreshing their relationship with God, some people have apparently come here to seek solitude in order to confront a tragedy in their life, rather than to specifically seek the heart of God.

I was reminded of how God can use pain in our lives to draw us to Him and also to further purify us. Isaiah 1:25 teaches us that God will "purge away our dross." The word in Hebrew for *"purge away"* is *tearaph*, which is the word used for smelting or refining. The term is usually used with refining fires, yet God is saying He will do it with lye. Lye is the closest thing the ancients had to soap. People knew nothing about microbes in those days, so they often didn't wash their hands unless they were about to touch something sacred. Because the ground was cursed (see Genesis 3:17), the ceremony of handwashing was done to remove anything on the hands that was cursed. Water was usually enough to do the cleansing, but at times you needed something a little stronger to really get the grit out; that was when lye was used.

While using lye might seem pretty harsh to us, the ancients did not have the luxury of using Ivory Soap or Irish Spring. At least cleansing by lye was not as rough as refining fires or the harsh, acidic chemicals used to refine silver. Although God sometimes uses the tragedies in our lives to bring us closer to Him, there are harsher methods He could employ. I suspect those who seek silence to recover from a difficult situation end up with a little bonus at the end of their retreat: they find a gentle cleansing of earthly passions in the loving-kindness of God.

4

THE MIGHTY TREE...AND THE THINGS THAT LAST

"For ye shall be as a terebinth whose leaf fadeth."
—Isaiah 1:30 (JPS Tanakh 1917)

I am beginning to think the abbey is built on a cemetery, considering all the gravesites there are on the property. I guess that when the brothers complete this life's journey, they are buried right on the grounds of the monastery. With the abbey being a hundred and fifty years old, that adds up to a lot of graves. This must be a constant reminder to the brothers here that our journey through this life is but a short one. We are just passing through, enjoying a few sights; our real destination is somewhere beyond the blue.

"For ye shall be as a terebinth whose leaf fadeth." The word in Hebrew for *"terebinth"* comes from the root word *'ayil,* among whose meanings is a mighty tree. All that this tree produces while it is alive dies in just a few short months, no matter how mighty it is. So what about all the "leaves" we produce in our lifetime, all of our accomplishments and achievements? When that memorial stone with our name on it is placed in the ground at our gravesite, what will all our imagined greatness be worth? As the old song I sang in Sunday school goes,

Only one life to offer.
Only one life that soon will pass.
Only what's done for Christ will last.[1]

---

1. Based on the poem "Only One Life, 'Twill Soon Be Past" by missionary C. T. Studd (1860–1931).

5

TREMBLING WITH SORROW

"Hear the word of the LORD, ye that tremble at his word."
—Isaiah 66:5

Last Sunday morning, when I was traveling to the abbey, I stopped off to worship at a church in Indiana. The leader of the congregation quoted Isaiah 66:5: *"Hear the word of the LORD, ye that tremble at his word."* This man of God said he had been so moved by the previous service that he trembled. When I hear the word *tremble*, I think of being so fearful that you are shaking in your boots. I cannot imagine that this church leader, who obviously loved God very much, would be fearful of God's words.

The word in Hebrew translated *"tremble"* in the above verse comes from the root word *charad*, which means to shake with great emotion—be it fear, sorrow, or pure joy. That leader did not say which emotion caused him to shake; perhaps he did not really know himself.

I am currently sitting in a prayer room looking out a window at the rolling hills of the Kentucky landscape, and I think of what it means to tremble with sorrow over someone else. On the window sill is a small sculpture of Jesus kneeling over the earth. His head is in His arms, and He is weeping over the world. The image is so lifelike, I can almost see Him shaking (*charad*) in His sorrow. Outside the window, sitting on the ledge, is a little mourning dove, cooing his mournful song. He is positioned right in front of the sculpture of the weeping Jesus, and I, too, have begun to weep. All three of us are expressing our mourning for the suffering of this world.

I am drawn closer to the heart of God to see what He is specifically weeping over. In my heart, I can see what my physical eyes do not see. I see Him holding the heart of a particular child. It is a young teenage girl, about thirteen or fourteen, whose name starts with a *K*. She has been hurt so deeply that she will not allow her heart to open in order to release the tears. The shell around her heart is so hard that no one can enter it, not even Jesus.

I look at Jesus as He holds this hardened heart, weeping over it. I reach out and lay my hand on His as it covers this precious little heart. Instantly, I begin to weep again. I say to Jesus, "Let me weep for her; let this dove's cooing soften this dear heart so that it will break open and release all those tears that have built up inside of it, so that she may cry out all that emotional hurt, pain, and sorrow. Then, when her heart has emptied of all its tears, You can fill it with the joy of Your heart."

As I weep with Jesus, and the mourning dove softly coos, I speak to this gentle heart, "Weep, my little K; weep until there are no more tears, and your heart will be filled with the love of God in Christ Jesus. Dear little K, I will likely never meet you in this world, but one day, we will meet in the world that is yet to come. When we do, I will tell you of your little dove, who flew to my window to lead a chorus of tears from the heart of Jesus, and how my heart joined with His, and how we all wept over your gentle heart that was so broken."

6

GIVE THANKS TO THE LORD

"I will give thanks unto the LORD according to His righteousness."
—Psalm 7:17 (JPS Tanakh 1917)

It is still a unique feeling to get up in the morning and know I don't have anything specific to do—no obligations, no expectations. The only thing there is to do, the only thing I have to do, is just be with Jesus and listen to the infinite sounds of His voice. In a sense, I hear His voice with my physical ears in every song being sung by His birds and in the sound of His wind blowing through the leaves. If I listen with my heart, I seem to hear them speak words from Scripture: *"I have loved you with an everlasting love"* (Jeremiah 31:3 NKJV). *"His name shall be called Wonderful, Counsellor, The mighty God, The everlasting Father, The Prince of Peace"* (Isaiah 9:6).

I feel prompted to look up Psalm 7:17, which says, *"I will give thanks unto the LORD according to His righteousness"* (JPS Tanakh 1917). The Hebrew word translated *"give thanks"* is *yadah.* The word is spelled yod, indicating a message from heaven; daleth, signifying a doorway; hei, designating God's presence. What *yadah* is telling me is that giving thanks is a doorway to God's presence. But soft, that word *yadah* has a secondary meaning, which is confession of sins. Am I still in the sin-confessing mode? I notice a robin sitting on a dying tree, but it is perched on one of the few branches that still has some green leaves on it. Perhaps Jesus is telling me that even in the midst of death, He will be found on whatever branch still has life. Where He goes, wherever He rests, there is always life, for He is life.

Birds are all around me now, but my attention is drawn to another robin hopping around on the ground. He suddenly jumps onto the branch of a dead tree and then looks at me. "Yeah, I get it," I say, "I am just a dead tree, and my ministry is really just a dead ministry. It is going to go nowhere." But then I realize that this tree is not dead—it is just a late bloomer. All the other trees are in bloom except this one. But its branches are filled with buds that will someday soon blossom into beautiful leaves. I think about the application for my own life. Even if it seems that all my former classmates from seminary now have ministries in full bloom, that doesn't mean my ministry is dead in comparison—it is just one that is a late bloomer. Since my ministry belongs to God, I will remember His love and His greatness, and I will give thanks as I sit in His presence, listening for His voice.

7

THE CALVARY ROAD

"Simon, sleepest thou? couldest not thou watch one hour?"
—Matthew 14:37

I am taking a walk through the woods, following a rustic trail that is supposed to lead to some statues. It is not an easy road, especially since I have a physical ailment. The trail has hills to climb and narrow bridges to cross. I guess this is supposed to remind us of the road that Jesus took to Calvary. I wonder what those statues will be like. Will they be of Jesus, or perhaps of the apostles, who also walked a hard road? Maybe they will be of some martyred saints who walked a difficult path for Jesus. Well, I will press on to find out.

The brothers have set up little shrines along the way so people walking the trail can stop and pray. For a sixty-two-year-old man, they are nice places to catch one's breath and take a little break. However, I think of how the Roman soldiers did not give Jesus a break when He walked that Calvary road, and He had been beaten beforehand. So I press on in the fellowship of His sufferings in my small, symbolic, but still rather painful, way.

Along the path, someone has left a little handwritten sign with Exodus 20:22 written on it: *"Then the LORD said to Moses, 'Thus you shall say to the sons of Israel, "You yourselves have seen that I have spoken to you from heaven"'"* (NASB). The person who left that note must have been convinced that God was going to speak to them on their little expedition to the statues. Actually, just seeing a portion of Scripture on this journey is having a real healing effect on me.

I arrive at a little shack that has a wooden sign on it saying, "Rosary House Shelter." Tacked all over the inside walls of this shelter are paper notes posted by other pilgrims. Each note reflects someone's soul cry. Some speak words of praise to God, such as "Jesus, You are great," or "I love You, Jesus." Some are more of a heart cry: "Heal me, O Lord." "Help me figure myself out." "Help me to forgive."

I find myself weeping again as I read these little messages addressed to God. Then I spot one that I know is the cry of a true servant of the Lord: "I have known hunger, loneliness, and thirst, and all was quenched by the Spirit of God; all is well, first things first." Indeed, first things first, and that is to find God's heart. So I now continue on my journey, wondering again what these statues will portray. I know and understand that I am on this little trip to hear God's heart cry to me. So I walk what I am now certain is a Calvary road.

I come to the first statue, which has this inscription on it: "May we always remember that the church exists to lead us to Christ in many and varied ways, but it is always the same Christ. —Gethsemane." I look up and see a sculpture of the disciples, asleep. I move a little further up the trail to another clearing, where there is a life-sized statue of Jesus on His knees, with His head back and His hands covering His face, expressing great anguish and agony. It is a depiction of the Savior praying in the garden of Gethsemane. I hear His heart speak. The church sleeps while Jesus suffers overwhelming agony and grief over a lost world. Can we not stay awake for a little while to hear the world's cry, and minister to the Master's grieving heart by finding those whom He mourns over and sharing His love with them?

It is now time for my return journey. I have made it to the statues, I have heard the message Jesus wanted me to hear, and I am stricken with grief. I sit down and weep over my still-callous attitude toward God's broken heart. But then His love floods me with an overwhelming sense of peace.

I still have the painful journey back to the abbey. I've read a number of adventures about people climbing mountains, like Mr. Everest. They all talk about the journey up but say little about the journey down. That, I think, would be the most hazardous part of an expedition, because you are already exhausted from the long climb up, but you have the same dangers going down. I will take it slowly.

8

STILL WATERS

"He leadeth me beside the still waters."
—Psalm 23:2

I am now having lunch with the brothers, in silence. They allow me to have my iPad so I can continue writing in my journal. I reflect on how I have hiked past both running waters and still waters today. I wonder why David specifically referenced *"still waters"* in Psalm 23:2 when he wrote, *"He leadeth me beside the still waters."* If I had my choice of drinking water, I would take the running water; *still waters* seem so stagnant. Besides, the flow of the running waters seems to create a coolness in their surroundings, producing a refreshing feeling. Still waters just sit there and bake in the hot sun.

The Hebrew word translated *"still"* in Psalm 23 is *manuchah*, which means rest or peace if it comes from the root word *manuch*. There is another possible root word, *nachan*, which means to give, as in a sacrifice. So a secondary meaning of this verse could be that God leads David beside *sacrificial giving waters*. The word for *"waters"* is *miy*, which can be either a noun or the interrogative *who*. I believe David carefully choose his words under the inspiration of God to give us two messages in one: Not only did he say that God leads us beside still waters (to bring us peace), but there is also a little play on words here in which he is saying, "He leads me to the One (Jesus) who will make a sacrificial gift (which will bring eternal peace)."

41

9

REFLECTIONS ON CLOUDS

*"And the LORD appeared in the tabernacle in a pillar of a cloud: and
the pillar of the cloud stood over the door of the tabernacle."*
—Deuteronomy 31:15

I'm sitting inside a screened porch because the bugs and I are not in harmony. Besides that, this Kentucky sun is brutal; I am used to a somewhat cooler climate. The porch is on the second floor overlooking the compound. As I look straight out, I can see the hills painted on the backdrop of blue sky and clouds. I cannot help but think of the old Peanuts comic strip in which Lucy, Linus, and Charlie Brown are looking at clouds, and Lucy asks the other two to relate the images they see. Linus sees a map of British Honduras, the profile of painter and sculptor Thomas Eakins, and the stoning of Stephen. Charlie Brown sees "a ducky and a horsie."

Indeed, many of us find it fascinating to look at clouds and their various formations. What we see in them can reveal something about how we perceive life, as it did for the Peanuts gang. Linus and Charlie Brown each saw something different in the same clouds, each eyeing a reflection of his inner thoughts. In fact, one of the words for "cloud" in Hebrew, 'anan, has that very connotation. This is the word that was used for the pillar of cloud by which the Israelites were guided by the Lord through the wilderness, the same cloud that appeared in the tabernacle. However, you will not find this meaning in your lexicon or in *Strong's Concordance*. Those resources will simply state that the word 'anan means cloud. But 'anan is spelled ayin, nun, nun. The ayin speaks to us of spiritual insight, and the nun signifies the number fifty. The sages teach that the number fifty represents the fiftieth gate to understanding. The double nun indicates a complete understanding. In fact, two nuns equal one hundred, which, according to Jewish literature, is the number of completion. Accordingly, what we see in clouds might bring us into an understanding of ourselves and of our relationship with God.

For instance, the cloud that I am looking at now looks like a galloping horse. No, I am not thinking of the Kentucky Derby, which will create havoc with the traffic on I-65 when I head home. Actually, I am thinking of the Hebrew word *soos*, which, in its noun form, means a horse, but which comes from the root idea of swift or speedy. That old cloud has brought to the surface my real concern: the sand in the hourglass is running out for me. I have been on this planet for three score and two years, and I feel as if I have accomplished so little for God. If He is going to do anything with my life, He'd better do it quickly!

10

A CLEAN HEART

"Create in me a clean heart, O God;
and renew a right spirit within me."
—Psalm 51:10

I went to the meditation room here at the abbey, and there were two chairs facing each other. It was as if two people had turned their chairs toward each other to carry on a conversation. But this could not be the case, because we are not to carry on any conversations in the meditation room. The idea is silence, after all. So how did the chairs end up facing each other? Either someone broke the rules, or someone else is having a good conversation with Jesus in the manner that I do. You see, when I really want a heart-to-heart conversation with Him, I will take two chairs and face them toward each other, and I will sit in one chair and imagine Jesus sitting in the other, and we will talk. But I usually arrange the chairs myself. This is the first time the chairs have already been facing each other. It is almost as if Jesus came ahead of me and rearranged the furniture, expecting to have this face-to-face talk. Of course, the idea that He or one of His angels came a few minutes before my arrival at the meditation room to set up the chairs is ridiculous, right? (Don't tell my study partner—she will say it was a miracle.)

Anyway, Jesus and I did talk. I reflected on the decades of my life and how God has always been faithful to direct my paths in relation to my life's vocations. Practically every job I have had is one I prayed for and God granted. And now, as I approach the final stage of my working life, I have only one more job I want to do. I have made this desire known to Him.

If He does not grant this one final vocational request, it will be a definite change in that pattern.

With that out of the way, we moved on to the next topic. There are still attitudes in my heart that I need to overcome. I told Him I was frustrated, that I had tried and tried, but I could not overcome these heart issues. He simply spoke to me Psalm 51:10: *"Create in me a clean heart."* I took a close look at the Hebrew word for *"create,"* and I found it was *bara*, the same word used in Genesis to describe God creating the heavens and the earth. God really did not do much actual creating, or *bara*-ing. He *bara*-ed the heavens and the earth, and the rest He called into being from that which He had already created. But He specializes in creating clean hearts. Thus, like David, I have asked Him for the creative miracle of a clean heart.

11

INNERMOST HEART

"Behold, Thou desirest truth in the inward parts; make me, therefore,
to know wisdom in mine inmost heart."
—Psalm 51:6 (JPS Tanakh 1917)

This morning, I went to the meditation room, and I again wept before Jesus. The tears came from very deep within me, but I didn't know if they were tears of joy, sadness, or repentance. I opened my Hebrew Bible and let my finger fall where it may, as I had on the first day I arrived. In fact, throughout this time of silence, I have been closing my eyes, opening my Hebrew Bible, and letting my finger fall to a verse. Each time, I have been led to a passage that addressed a specific question I had or the issue I was dealing with. I seem to be doing this without a second thought and not being at all surprised when the verse matches my question or issue.

As I asked Jesus why I was weeping, I let my finger fall to a verse that happened to be Psalm 51:6: *"Behold, Thou desirest truth in the inward parts; make me, therefore, to know wisdom in mine inmost heart."* My eyes rested on those words *"inmost heart."* David is not just asking for wisdom in his heart, but in his *innermost* heart. As Shakespeare said in Hamlet, "In my heart's core, ay, in my heart of heart."[2]

I believe that the tabernacle in the wilderness, and later the temple in Israel, were designed to be a picture of our heart. In these structures, there was the outer court, where all were welcomed, even Gentiles. That is like the outer layer of our heart, where we welcome loved ones, friends, and

---

2. *Hamlet*, Act III, Scene II.

strangers alike. Then there was the inner court, where only those who were true worshippers of God could enter; this was where the priest offered the sacrifices to God. The inner court corresponds to the inner layer of our heart, the area where we are more selective about who gets in—only true loved ones, such as spouses and other immediate family members, are permitted to go into that layer of our heart. It is where we enter into intimacy with the ones in those special relationships, where we sacrifice for those relationships, and where we share our joy and sorrow. Believers also allow Jesus to enter this inner court of their hearts.

Yet, there was one other area of the tabernacle or temple that was even more select; it was the area that only one person, the high priest, was allowed to enter, and that only once a year on the Day of Atonement, for it was the Holy of Holies, the place where the presence of God Himself resided. Similarly, our heart has a "holy of holies," an innermost part, the core of our heart. We usually allow only one Person—God—to enter that chamber of our heart.

In Psalm 51:6, the Hebrew word translated *"inmost heart"* is *satham*. In its most primitive form, *satham* refers to the "secret place" of the heart. David wanted to know *wisdom* in this most secret, private place of his heart. Why wisdom? The word in Hebrew for *"wisdom"* in this verse comes from the root word *chakam*, meaning to be wise. The first letter in *chakam* is chet. The sages teach us that, as two horizontal lines connected by a vertical line, the chet represents a bridge between two hearts—our heart and God's heart. The next letter is kap, which we are told is a vessel, such as our heart, that needs to be filled. In the case of wisdom, or *chakam*, it needs to be filled with what the last letter, the final mem, symbolizes. This letter represents the hidden knowledge, or the secrets, of God. Thus, David is inviting God to share the innermost part of his own heart, his holy of holies, desiring that God would, in turn, share the innermost part of His heart, His Holy of Holies, His secrets, with him.

In this little meditation room, Jesus and I struck a deal: I would share my *satham*, the inner core of my heart, with Him, if He would share the inner core of His heart, His secrets, with me. This does come with a price, for if I am to explore the depths of His heart, I must allow Him to explore the secrets of my heart. How long has it been since I have done that? Have I ever purposely allowed Him to explore the depths of my heart?

12

AN EMPTY HEART

"And the LORD God called unto Adam,
and said unto him, Where art thou?"
—Genesis 3:9

I am sitting alone in the balcony of the chapel. The brothers were here earlier, having arrived at 3:30 a.m. to pray. Some are now off making their cheese, fudge, and pottery, which they will sell to support the abbey. Others are tending to the garden where they grow fruits and vegetables to supplement their diet. Later, the brothers will have some free time to indulge in their many and varied hobbies, such as astronomy (there is a small observatory on the compound equipped with a telescope). Some will study, some will paint or sculpt, and some will even practice a musical instrument. Yet they will do all as unto the Lord in an attitude of prayer, for they practice prayer without ceasing, and they do so in silence, without speaking.

In this sanctuary are many small wooden benches for the individual brothers, each with its own podium across from it. Some of the brothers have left their prayer books at their places. Later, they will all return to pray again, when they will join their voices in a beautiful chant of praise and worship.

The sanctuary is clean, spotless, held sacred—yet now empty. The atmosphere echoes what I am feeling. Jesus has allowed me to enter the heart of His heart, and I find it very lonely in here. A brother just walked into the chapel, passing through. He pauses long enough to honor the host and then leaves. He is simply in the midst of going about his day, but the action reminds me of so many of us Christians—we pop in and out of God's heart, pausing long enough to give our respects but never staying around for an extended visit. Few believers really enter His heart of hearts, and usually only on special occasions.

Jesus is reminding me about how often we just skim the surface of His heart. A quick "Praise the Lord," or a "Thank You for this food," and we are off gratifying our own desires, wants, and needs, leaving behind this Lover who has prepared a special room for us in which to remain and converse, to have a meal of the Bread of Life and a chance to feast on His Word. No, instead, we have to switch on the ball game lest we miss an important play.

I can sense the ache in Jesus's heart, and He seems to be saying, "I have prepared a feast for My loved ones, yet they are too busy with their lives to spend time with Me. Did you know that many of My churches actually delayed, shortened, or even cancelled their services on Super Bowl Sunday? I prepared this place for each one, with a special feast, but they did not want to miss the kickoff." Jesus wept. I wept, too, for He was exploring my heart and showing me the many times I myself was *too busy* to talk with my Lord, my special Friend.

I said, "Lord, but there are millions and millions of believers around the world. Would I really be missed?" I then thought of an interview I had seen on television with the mother of twelve children who had lost one of them to gang violence. As she wept, the reporter reminded her that she had eleven other children. She responded, "Yes, but it still hurts just as bad as if he were an only child."

I thought of the brothers here at the abbey who gather together for their morning prayers, day after day, month after month—praying together, singing together, chanting together. This morning, I listened to their voices during my time of meditation; they had all sung in unison, in perfect harmony, as they have been doing for years. If just one of those brothers did not show up one day, he would be missed; the morning prayers would not be the same. Oh, they would go on, but it just would not sound the same.

I look out again over the empty sanctuary, and I understand why Jesus has led me here. He has explored my heart and found that there are other desires, interests, and concerns that are more important to me than He is. I realize that this vacant place of worship symbolizes what God's inner heart feels like if I am too busy for Him. Oh, sure, there are others who will enter His inner heart. But He is like that mother who lost her child—even though she has eleven other children still alive, her house feels empty with that one child missing. Thus, God's inner heart may have many of His children worshipping in it, but if just one of His beloved is missing, His heart longs for that absent one.

13

IN THE WILDERNESS

"For thus said the Lord God, the Holy One of Israel:
In sitting still and rest shall ye be saved,
in quietness and in confidence shall be your strength."
—Isaiah 30:15 (JPS Tanakh 1917)

It is about an hour before lunch. I am lying on my bunk, yet I cannot really rest, because every moment is important on this retreat. I think of Matthew 4:1: *"Then was Jesus led up of the Spirit into the wilderness…."* Jesus spent forty days in silence in the wilderness. The King James Version says that He was *"led up [there] of the Spirit."* This phrase would more accurately be translated from the Greek and Aramaic as "led up *by* the spirit." Additionally, although most Bible versions capitalize the word "Spirit," the text does not indicate which *spirit*. The Aramaic uses the word *roka*, which is generally used to express the Holy Spirit or the Spirit of God. That would be Jesus's own Spirit, for although Jesus had a body and (if we hold to a tripartite view) a soul, His Spirit was the Spirit of God Himself. The Spirit of God dwelled within Jesus. Today, that same Spirit dwells within us if we have accepted God's gift of salvation. I believe it is this same Spirit who has led me to spend a week in silence at this monastery.

Matthew 4:1 says that Jesus was led by the Holy Spirit into the *"wilderness."* The Aramaic word for "wilderness" is *madbra*, which means a desert; a desolate place; a wild, arid region without inhabitants. That is not exactly the kind of place where the Holy Spirit has led me, but I think my stay at the abbey has had an effect on me similar to being in a wilderness. I could not have lived in silence like this at home. I might have spent this week off from work just hanging around my apartment, but there still would have been distractions to divert me from my purpose. The Internet, TV, nearby shopping areas—any number of things could have drawn me away and taken my mind off of my meditations for a few moments or even hours.

Right now, I feel a temptation to hop in my car and go to the town about fifteen miles away to purchase a pair of sunglasses, because I could really use them here. Yet to do that would seem to interrupt a certain flow of the Spirit of God. I don't fully understand it all, but I do realize that there is something significant about spending time in *madbra*, where God can have one's undivided attention for a length of time. I find that even while I am lying on my bunk, having exhausted all my prayers—everything I wanted to say to God—the Spirit of God is ministering something to me.

As I approach the lunch hour, I don't feel like going outside; I don't feel like taking a walk; I don't even feel like praying or studying the Word of God—I need a break from all of that. I could pull up a book on my iPad to read, maybe a good novel. Or I could plug the earphones into my iPad and listen to an audiobook, a sermon, or a teaching I have downloaded, or perhaps listen to music. Or I could just take a nap. There's nothing wrong with any of those things. But I can do them fifty-one weeks out of the year. This is God's week, my week in *madbra*, where there is a flow of the Spirit of God that I do not want to interrupt.

So what should I do? Maybe the same thing a couple does on their honeymoon or on their second honeymoon, when, after a day of sightseeing, eating out, and walking along a beach holding hands and talking, they have run out of things to do and say, so they just settle down and hold each other, not saying a word. Perhaps now is the time for God and me to just hold each other, not saying a word but simply enjoying each other's presence. The people from the Toronto Blessing call this *soaking*, and the ancient Jewish sages called it *devek*, a clinging to God, a "hugging" of God and letting Him hug you. You don't need to express a word; you can just rest in the embrace.

14

PREPARING OUR HEART

"That they might set their hope in God, and not forget the works of God, but keep his commandments: and might not be as their fathers, a stubborn and rebellious generation; a generation that set not their heart aright, and whose spirit was not stedfast with God."
—Psalm 78:7–8

God has led me to Psalm 78:8, which recalls a rebellious nation *"that set not their heart aright."* The Hebrew word translated as *"set...aright"* is *kuwn,* one of whose meanings is to prepare. The Israelites did not prepare their hearts for God.

This psalm is describing Israel during the time of the Exodus, when God did some truly remarkable miracles, and yet the people were not satisfied. Every day, there was the miracle of manna from heaven that nourished them in the desert, and yet the people wanted something different. They wanted variety in their diet—meat, fruits, vegetables. Surely God wanted them to prosper. Why should they settle for plain old manna?

Just as I am ready to throw rocks at the Israelites for their ingratitude, God essentially shouts out to me, "Hold it—before you talk of that speck in your brother's eye, how about that board in your own eye?" (See, for example, Matthew 7:4 NKJV.)

I suddenly thought of an article I had read about the president of a major movie studio, a multimillionaire who daily rubbed shoulders with the rich and powerful. He was on location in a Third World country and was visiting a garbage dump where children were picking through the trash, searching for food or something they could sell to gain a little money. At that moment, he received a call on his cell phone from the agent of a famous movie star, who was having a meltdown because his private jet did not have certain amenities that he had ordered. He overheard this movie star in the background, screaming and saying that he did not have to live like this. This executive then looked out at the children digging in the garbage dump to find something that would help their families to survive, and he decided right then and there to resign from his position, move to this Third World country, and use his wealth to build a school and a medical clinic.

Unfortunately, I believe I am like that movie star and the Israelites in the desert. I have so much from God, yet I am never satisfied. I keep wanting more. I think about my earlier conversation with the Lord regarding my vocational request. I am not satisfied with what He has already given me. After all, He is a rich God, so why would He not want to give me the best? Why would He not want me to live in comfort and prosperity? I really don't have to live like this!

Have I not learned anything during my time of silence? Has He not shown me the cross and His suffering on that cross?

No, my problem is not greed. It is the same problem that the people of Israel faced—they had not *kuwn*-ed, or *prepared*, their hearts for the miracles that would come. If we don't have a prepared heart, miracles will only spoil our soul. Maybe my call to this week of silence is to prepare me for miracles that will follow. If it is, I must "set my heart aright" so that if and when they do come, my soul will not be spoiled and unsatisfied. I will need to learn to accept each miracle from God as possibly the only or last miracle I will ever receive from Him, and be grateful.

There is an old story of a servant woman who was washing dishes and praying, thinking she was alone. She prayed, "O Lord, if I only had five hundred dollars, I would be the most satisfied woman in the world." The master of the house overheard this and went in and told her he had heard her prayer and that he would give her the five hundred dollars. After he left, he put his ear to the door to listen to her next prayer, of thanks to God. However, her next prayer was, "Lord, why didn't You make me say one thousand dollars?"

I know—some preachers would say I should think big, as big as I can, and then ask God for a great request. But if I am learning anything from this time of silence, it is that I do not need to think big; I only need to think God.

15

A HANDFUL OF QUIETNESS

"Better is a handful of quietness than two hands full
of toil and a striving after wind."
—Ecclesiastes 4:6 (ESV)

In the verse above, the Hebrew word translated as *"striving"* comes from the root word *ra'ah*, which can mean "a consuming passion." The word rendered *"better"* is *tov*, which denotes being in harmony with God. The word for *"quietness"* is *nachath*, which means just that—quietness. *Nachath* is spelled nun, chet, taw. The nun represents productivity in relation to the chet, which symbolizes a bonding with God and a joining of our hearts with His heart; this results in the taw, which speaks of truth and praise leading to repair and restoration. In quietness with God, we produce more than we do with our labors, which can become a consuming passion and a chasing after the wind that will only pass away. What is accomplished in quietness is everlasting; the product of our quietness endures for eternity.

This word study reminds me that I have seen many ministries that were built solely upon a person and their name. Little effort was made to grow these ministries in quietness, which means to grow them according to the heart of God. Their growth came only from name recognition. Their leaders or followers exalted the name of the founder and essentially tithed to the founder, although, for the sake of "religious correctness," they said they were tithing to God. The evidence that a ministry is merely the result of labors filled with a consuming passion for temporary things is that after the founder dies, the ministry flounders. Attempts are made to keep the organization going, and many such ministries do continue, due to the hiring of business consultants and business managers who can keep a ministry going, just as they might keep any business going.

Then there are ministries that both continue *and* flourish after their founder dies. I was recently listening on the radio to the teaching of a minister who passed away over twenty years ago. He still teaches through his recorded messages, and all his messages are simple instruction on and from the Bible itself. The ministry he founded was one that grew in quietness, or *nachath*. I am praying that my little ministry will be modeled after that one. It will be a simple ministry of the Word of God. It will be built on a desire to know and study the Scriptures, and my name will not be found anywhere, even in its articles of incorporation.

Uh-oh, I feel Jesus's penetrating gaze. I ask, "But Lord, are You not impressed that I want a ministry to be built on *nachath*?" Jesus's response is that all ministries were *built* on *nachath*, but once the power, fame, and wealth entered, another name took over. "Well, Jesus," I continue, "You have nothing to worry about; my ministry will never grow to the point where it will have power, fame, and wealth. It will just be a nice little homespun ministry." This time, Jesus's response is, "That is what concerns Me." I will need to meditate on that one.

16

IN HIS LIKENESS

"As for me, I will behold thy face in righteousness: I shall be satisfied,
when I awake, with thy likeness."
—Psalm 17:15

In Psalm 17, David says he will *"behold"* God's face. In Hebrew, this is the word *chazah*, which, in its root form, means to experience. David will experience God's presence in righteousness; He will experience God's presence when he is doing the right thing.

I believe I am beginning to understand. I have been experiencing God's presence in these days of silence, but there are times when my thoughts shift away from Him, and I begin thinking about other things. I become aware that I am not doing what is right because I suddenly no longer feel His presence. After pondering this idea, I read the rest of Psalm 17:15. It says that David will be satisfied to awaken with God's likeness. The Hebrew word translated *"likeness"* is *temonah*, which basically means to be in someone's image, not so much physically but in actions and personality.

I recently heard a preacher who was a guest speaker at a congregation. He was very much a *temonah*. The way he combed his hair, the way he preached with a lot of shouting, the jokes he told, and his general humor were so similar to those of dozens of other preachers I have heard. The people still laughed, still applauded, still got excited, even though he was pressed from the same cookie cutter as all the others.

A few weeks ago, I heard a different preacher who was also a *temonah*. However, he spoke from his heart, which you could tell was actually his heart joined with God's. He did not shout or tell jokes. He simply talked about the love of God and how he was satisfied to just know Jesus and His sacrifice on the cross. That was enough; that was all he really needed. To me, this man was in the likeness, or *temonah*, of Jesus.

It has been said that the greatest form of flattery is when someone imitates you. Maybe imitating Christ will not draw the big crowds, but it will bring great *saba*, or satisfaction. I will be satisfied to awaken with His likeness.

17

STILL SHINING BRIGHTLY

"Who commands the sun, and it does not rise;
who seals up the stars."
—Job 9:7 (ESV)

I don't get to see the stars too much here at the abbey. Since 3:15 a.m. is the wake-up time, and since the bells ring for Compline at 7:30 p.m., most of the retreatants, including me, are in bed by the time the stars come out. But this morning, before 3:15, I did have a chance to catch the stars as they served as a backdrop to the Kentucky hills. There sure are a lot of them!

The Bible tells us in Job 9:7 that God can seal up the stars at His command. The Hebrew word translated *"seals"* is *chatam*, which means to lock up or to stop. In the context of this verse, it means to cause the sun (which is a star) to *stop shining*. I have read books on astronomy that explain how many stars that appear in our sky actually burned out centuries ago, but their light was so bright, and it has taken so long for that light to travel to us, that we are still seeing their radiance today.

God allows us to continue to see the light of a burned-out star just as He allows us to keep seeing the light of believers whose lives "burned out" years ago—at least their lives on this earth. D. L. Moody's light keeps shining through the school he built over one hundred years ago, which has never moved from its solid doctrinal position and is still training hundreds of future pastors, missionaries, and Christian workers every year.

Likewise, George Mueller passed on to heaven over one hundred years ago, but his light still shines through the children's homes that he started and the legacy of the faith that built them. Even today, many believers read and hear about the faith of Mueller, who never asked for a penny from anyone to support his ministry to orphaned and destitute children. He went solely to God in prayer and trusted Him to provide—and He did. Christians today are, and Christians in the future will continue to be, encouraged and challenged by the example and light of Mueller's remarkable faith.

Additionally, there is a long list of other believers who have gone on to heaven whose light still burns brightly as an example to us all. As I begin yet another day of silence, my prayer is that my light will continue to shine brightly even after I join the other followers of Jesus in "that great getting' up mornin'."[3] May it shine as an encouragement to the faith of believers in the future who will be traveling on their own life journeys in this physical world.

---

3. Mahalia Jackson, "Great Gettin' Up Morning," 1959. Lyrics © Warner/Chappell Music, Inc.

18

OUR SPIRIT IS LISTENING

*"So shall my word be that goeth forth out of my mouth: it shall not
return unto me void, but it shall accomplish that which I please, and it
shall prosper in the thing whereto I sent it."*
—Isaiah 55:11

I am told that the pretzel was invented by monks, and its shape is that of
arms crossed and folded over the chest or heart. That was the posture
the brothers encouraged me to assume during Communion. As I am not
Catholic, I am not permitted to partake of the elements here at the abbey.
However, I was informed that by folding my arms across my chest or heart
in prayer, I receive the body and blood of Christ in my spirit, which is, after
all, the whole point and purpose of Communion.

Additional practices of the brothers interest me. They pause seven
times throughout the day to pray, although they are always in an attitude
of contemplative prayer. During these seven periods of prayer—known as
Vigils, Lauds, Terce, Sext, None, Vespers, and Compline—they pray from
the Psalms. By this exercise, they go through all one hundred and fifty
psalms every two weeks. I know that by praying this way seven times a day,
week after week, month after month, the practice could become merely
routine or an empty ritual. But then, many Protestant Christians I know
doggedly get up every morning and struggle through a half hour of quiet
time; they try to perform at least thirty minutes of praying and reading
from the Word of God. Is that not a ritual? Additionally, some will play
an audio recording of Scripture being read as they go about their business, paying little attention to what they are hearing. Furthermore, their

children are encouraged to memorize Scripture in Sunday school to obtain little prizes. Many of the children do not understand what they are memorizing; they just like getting the rewards. Are these practices not ritual?

Yet when the chips are down and you do not have a Bible handy, how many times does a Scripture verse you don't even remember reading or hearing come back to you? Do not the Scriptures teach in Isaiah 55:11 that God's Word will not return to Him void? The Hebrew word translated "*void*" in that verse is *reyqam*, which means to be without any effect. Thus, what God speaks is always effective; it will "*accomplish*" and "*prosper in*" His purposes. (See verse 11.) And does it not say in Hebrews 4:12 that God's Word is "*sharper than any two-edged sword*" (NASB, NKJV, ESV)?

The Word of God is potent and fruitful. Consider the difference between God's Word and other types of literature. For example, if someone were to stand up and begin to quote Shakespeare, I might not understand a word they are saying, and I might become bored with it. In such a case, I doubt if I would remember any of what I heard. In contrast, as the brothers chant the Psalms, I have a hard time following what they are saying, but I know it is the Word of God, and I am almost brought to tears just hearing the Scriptures, even though I cannot really make out the exact portion of Scripture they are reciting. Furthermore, if I got in a tight spot, I probably would not start quoting Shakespeare for comfort. But the Word of God comes very quickly to my mind and brings me comfort and peace during difficult times. The difference between Shakespeare and the Word of God is that there is power, as well as the very presence of God, embedded in His Word. I can physically feel something when the Word of God is spoken. Cleansing and healing waves flow over me when God's Word is expressed.

Much of what the brothers here practice in their religious order is out of the scope of my persuasion—I am, after all, still a Baptist at heart. However, I cannot deny that there is a certain peace, serenity, and contentment about the brothers. You may say it is their lifestyle, in which they are free from the pressures and stresses of modern life. For the most part, I would agree. Still, I cannot help but believe that a lot of that peace comes from being exposed continually to the power of the Word of God. The Word of God truly has a purifying effect on our hearts.

I remember reading a story in the Talmud about a student who complained about another student to his rabbi, saying that this student studied the Torah only in order to become so knowledgeable that people would be impressed with his learning and say flattering things about him. The rabbi replied, "Don't worry, the Torah will purify his motives."

I suppose reciting Scripture over and over can become a ritual, and maybe playing an audio recording of Scripture being read is just ritual, too. Yet there is something peaceful and joyful in listening to Scripture being spoken, even if you do not fully comprehend what you are hearing or are not even paying attention to it. In such cases, our minds might be otherwise occupied, but our spirits are listening very intently. Later that day, week, or month, or perhaps even years from now, you may find yourself quoting a Scripture verse and wonder where it came from. It came from your spirit, which had been listening closely while your flesh was preoccupied.

19

A BIRTHDAY *DEVEK*

"Ye shall serve him, and cleave unto him."
—Deuteronomy 13:4

Happy spiritual birthday to me. Fifty years ago today, I was born again. I did not plan to spend my golden anniversary with Jesus in silence; it just happened that way. I suppose it is just a coincidence, although, to use a good Pentecostal term, maybe it is a God-incidence. As someone once said, "It is funny how, when I pray, coincidences happen; and when I stop praying, coincidences stop happening."

Being cloistered away in silence, it is very unlikely that I will celebrate this birthday at Chuck E. Cheese's or some other entertainment establishment. Instead, it will be a time of quiet reflection on fifty years of a growing relationship with the Jesus whom I have learned to dearly love. The joy I felt that day fifty years ago, I still feel today, only it is even richer, purer, deeper, and sweeter than it was then. Jesus has been my dearest Friend down through the years. This old ship of my life has been through many a storm in the last half century. It has been beaten and battered; its mast is shredded, its rudder is broken, and its hull is taking in water. But the Rock that it is anchored to still holds—my Rock still holds.

Another retreatant just walked by, sobbing rather loudly. Aren't we supposed to be silent? I guess the expressions of the heart are exempt from that rule. It is strange how being touched by God often expresses itself in tears. In this environment, no one appears to notice when someone is weeping; we all pay it no mind, although it does seem somehow callous.

But what is happening is usually a God thing, and He is better able to deal with it than we are. Besides, what would we say? We are not allowed to speak.

I sense Jesus calling me to a *devek*, that clinging to God, that hugging of God and letting Him hug you, which I described earlier. *"Ye shall walk after the* Lord *your God, and fear him, and keep his commandments, and obey his voice, and ye shall serve him, and cleave unto him"* (Deuteronomy 13:4). The Hebrew word translated *"cleave"* is *devek*. This concept is very important to the Orthodox Jew. It is like a child clinging to their mother or father out of pure love, not wanting to let go, desiring to just stay in that parent's arms forever. Or it is like two lovers who go off to a secret place, shut out the world, and just hold each other, finding joy and rest in each other's embrace. We are to walk with God, to reverence Him, to keep His commandments, to obey His voice, to serve Him, and to *hug* Him.

So, if you will excuse me, I feel God calling me to a secret, private place where He can give me my birthday hug. Of course, I shall hug Him in return, and we will spend a few hours just holding each other, saying nothing, just enjoying each other's presence.

20

WORSHIP

"Worship the LORD in the beauty of holiness."
—Psalm 29:2

People have different ideas about what worship is. To the brothers here at the abbey, worship takes the form of liturgy and ceremony. To a Baptist, worship means sitting for about an hour in church, singing a few praise songs or hymns, and listening to a pastor who has been to Bible college and seminary tell us what the Word of God says. To a Pentecostal, worship is enthusiastic singing, clapping, raising one's hands, and dancing. Actually, none of these things is worship; it is just an expression of worship, or a by-product of worship.

The Hebrew word translated *"worship"* in Psalm 29:2 is *shachah*. I have found the same word in other Semitic languages. Lexicons say it means to bow down or to fall prostrate. But this word is so much more than that. *Shachah* is spelled shin, chet, hei. The letter shin tells us that in worship, God encompasses us with His passionate love. The chet signifies that in worship, God uses His passionate love to bridge the gap between us and Him so that He can surround us with His hei, or His presence.

Actually, the Hebraic origins of *shachah* indicate that worship is more passive on our part and more active on God's part. God really does all the work in worship. Somehow, we get the idea that we have to sing, dance, and shout to obtain God's presence. But again, these are just the by-products or the results of worship. Worship is simply giving yourself to God 100 percent. Worship means standing, sitting, bowing, or falling prostrate before

God and saying, "I am Yours; find whatever pleasure You can in me." In return, we are filled with great joy over knowing that the God whom we love has found pleasure in us. We are awed that we have such worth in God's eyes that the Creator of the universe actually wants to be in relationship with us and draws pleasure from little old unworthy us. Such an experience can only cause us to whoop for joy and swing from the rafters!

Shachah has its roots in a Ugaritic[4] word. I remember translating a Ugaritic poem about a goddess who fell in love with a mortal man and had an intimate relationship with him. The word used to describe this relationship was a form of the word *shachah*. The ancient concept of *shachah* was that of a god sharing his or her passion with a human being, and the human sharing his or her passion with the god. But in the Hebrew sense of worship, *shachah* signifies spiritual passion and oneness between God and His people.

In a marriage relationship, the true joy of intimacy is to bring pleasure to your spouse. Of course, if that is also your spouse's intention for you, then you will receive pleasure in return. This creates sort of an O'Henry "Gift of the Magi," in which the gift turns out to be irrelevant in light of the love behind it. That is *shachah*; that is worship.

God created the marriage relationship to teach us about our relationship with Him. However, if you were merely to use your wife or husband in order to bring pleasure to yourself, then you would not be demonstrating the love of God; essentially, you would be reducing your spouse to the level of a prostitute. Likewise, if we engage in worship only to bring pleasure to ourselves, what are we saying about our relationship with God? For example, if we turn to God only in order to receive prosperity and comfort from Him, then we are not treating Him like a beloved husband but rather using Him like a sugar daddy.

During this week that I have spent in silence, I have not sung one praise song or attended one service with a worship team that uses guitars, drums, or other instruments. Neither have I danced or shouted or swung from the rafters (definitely not in that two-story-high chapel). But I have

---

4. Ugaritic is a Northwest Semitic language whose grammatical features are highly similar to that of the Hebrew grammar. The Ugaritic language has been used by scholars of the Hebrew Bible to clarify biblical Hebrew texts.

worshipped God. In fact, my whole time in silence has been a period of worship in which I have just allowed God to take pleasure in me. I have let Him have me all to Himself with no distractions. Can you fathom it? Me! Sinful, flawed piece of humanity me, yet somehow the God of the universe has managed to find pleasure in this old slob of a person. I just have to tell you, wonders never cease. You want a miracle, that is one right there—that this all-powerful, all-knowing God would take pleasure in the likes of me. I mean, you would think He could do better, maybe someone like Billy Graham. Still, He created me, so He will just have to take what He created.

Yet God continues to work on me. One of the brothers here at the abbey is a potter, and I went and watched him work. He must have built one single lump of clay into a vessel a dozen times. Each time, he apparently felt there was some flaw in the vessel, and therefore he kept smashing it back down into a lump until, at last, he raised it up to become the vessel he wanted. God spoke to me as I watched this, and you can easily guess what He was telling me. (It was reminiscent of Jeremiah's experience in Jeremiah 18.) I am like a lump of clay that He is building up but has to keep smashing down again every time He finds a flaw. He must continue doing this until I become that perfect vessel that He longs to possess.

As I think about my soon return to everyday life, I know that people will ask me, "Well, what did God do for you in your week of silence? What did you get from God?" I am afraid I will have to reply that I "got" nothing. God got all the pleasure in having me completely to Himself for a week. However, in return, I found great joy in bringing pleasure to the One I love.

I am reminded of the time when I worked in an office. For each employee's birthday, the office manager would take a collection from the other employees to purchase some doughnuts or a cake in honor of that person. One time, a supervisor's birthday was somehow overlooked. The next day, he came to the office with a big box of doughnuts. I asked him what the occasion was, and he said he had purchased it for us for his birthday. Well, seeing that it is my spiritual birthday, it is I who am purchasing the "doughnuts" for God to enjoy.

21

GOD'S DELIGHT AND DESIRE

"How fair and how pleasant art thou, O love, for delights!… I am my beloved's, and his desire is toward me."
—Song of Solomon 7:6, 10

How *fair and how pleasant art thou, O love, for delights!"* Oh, come now, King James Version—you can be a little more romantic than that! The words *"how pleasant art thou, O love"* are translated from one compound word in the Hebrew: *na'amethe'ahavah*. Minus the vowels, the word has eight letters, which is a long word in Hebrew. It combines the words *n'ameth'a* (pleasurable) and *ahavah* (feminine love). Literally, what Solomon is saying here to the peasant woman with whom he has fallen in love is, "Your love is such a pleasure." This is how God speaks to us when we love Him. As I expressed earlier, our love is a great joy to Him. Simply loving Him brings Him pleasure, or *n'ameth'a*.

This word depicts the pleasure that comes from feasting on some delicacy. It might be a "comfort food," like chocolate cake or ice cream—something that you rarely allow yourself to indulge in, but when you do, you savor every bite. Likewise, if you have ever been on a diet, you probably know *n'ameth'a* very well. After steering clear of sweets for a while, simply to taste one piece of chocolate brings you into a land of pleasure and satisfaction, and you experience an overall good feeling. When we love God, it brings Him this type of pleasure.

In Song of Solomon 7:6, the words *"for delights"* are translated from another long word in Hebrew; that word also has eight letters, buried in plurals, prepositions, and articles. The root word is *'anag*, which is something so fragile, so delicate, that you want to cuddle it, coo to it, and protect it. It is like a puppy whose sad little eyes make you want to reach out to hold it and kiss it. Or it is like a bride who has made herself completely vulnerable to her bridegroom such that he wants to wrap his arms around her, hold her, whisper sweet words of love to her, and protect her from any storm, danger, or even insult. That is what it means when God says that He delights in us.

But there is even more to learn in this passage about God's powerful love for us. In Song of Solomon 7:10, Solomon's betrothed says, "*I am my beloved's, and his desire is toward me.*" The first phrase is, "*I am my beloved's.*" I'll say it again: is that the best the translator could do? I am convinced that this verse was rendered by some grumpy old scholar sitting in his self-contained academic tower who hadn't kissed his wife in twenty years. Hebrew is an emotional language, and what we need are poets, people like Elizabeth Barrett Browning, involved in some of our translations.

The above rendering totally ignores the presence of the preposition lamed. It should really say, "I am *for* my beloved." That is to say, "I *belong* to my beloved." The Hebrew word translated "*beloved*" is *dodi*. This word conveys the idea of two people holding hands. The ancients believed that your heart was in the palm of your right hand. Thus, when you shook hands in those days, it meant you were sharing your heart with that person. So Solomon's beloved is actually saying that her heart belongs to him, her lover.

But she also adds, "*His desire is toward me.*" The word translated "*toward*" is *'al*, which really means "over." Thus, it is as if his desire for her is poised over her head and is present with her wherever she goes. Actually, to say it is his *desire* that is suspended over her is putting it mildly. The Hebrew word translated "*desire*" comes from the root word *shuq*, which indicates a desperate desire, a longing or a craving, even an addiction. This is a desire that is so powerful you can actually feel it emanating from someone. Therefore, the little peasant woman whom Solomon loves actually feels his desire for her, and it is always present with her.

Could God really have such a desire for us? Could He actually have a longing for us that is so strong we could feel it? After spending these days in silence, I can only say yes. In silence, I have felt a strong pull toward the Jesus whom I love. I have felt His overwhelming desire to just let me put my head on His shoulder, to weep out all those years of pain and heartbreak, to share my years of disappointments and failures, and then to have me hear Him gently whisper, "It's okay." And you know what? When He says it is okay, it really is okay. To have come through all those years and still have the same faith I had fifty years ago, that alone makes it all okay. Those years are behind me now, and what is ahead is a day when I will see Him face-to-face.

Jesus's parable of the prodigal son expresses the longing that God the Father has for us. Hebrew oral tradition also has a prodigal son story, one that Hebrew mothers probably told their children at bedtime. As a good rabbi, Jesus retold this story that was so familiar to His disciples; however, in His version, the father did something different than he did in the original story. He did not just say to his son, who had run away from home, "Come toward home as far as you can, and I will meet you." In Jesus's retelling of it, the father runs down the road toward his wayward son, filled with *shuq*, or longing. Reaching his son, he throws his arms around him, hugs him, and kisses him. (See Luke 15:11–32.)

In the last few days, I have met such a heavenly Father; I have felt His arms around me, and I have experienced His embrace and His *devek*. I can now truly say that this is the reason God called me to silence. As I am about to conclude this week and pack my bags to leave this place of solitude and return to a noisy, confusing world, I wonder again what I will say when people ask, "Well, how was it?" What can I tell them? I had no vision of heaven; I did not see any pearly gates, streets of gold, or mansions. Yet, in silence, I have learned what heaven is like, and it is glorious. In silence, I have found a place that is filled with God's love, passion, and overwhelming desire and longing to give me a never-ending *devek*.

22

OUR HEART'S DESIRE

"The LORD is nigh unto them that are of a broken heart."
—Psalm 34:18

The book of Hebrews tells us that *"faith is the substance of things hoped for, and the evidence of things not seen"* (Hebrew 11:1). The word for "hope" in the Aramaic means "a positive imagination." Being a good Semite, the writer might have had that word in mind when he wrote this verse. If so, it would read something like this: "Faith is the substance of your positive imagination and the evidence of things not seen." The most positive thing I can imagine is Jesus, and He, of course, is Someone I cannot see. Therefore, every day in my call to silence, I have gone to the meditation room, and, as I described earlier, I have faced an empty chair, imagining Jesus sitting across from me. By faith, I have been having an ongoing conversation with Him.

Today was our final time together in the meditation room. Jesus asked me once again what I wanted. I told Him how foolish I had been on my first day of silence. I was filled with all sorts of expectations—anticipating seeing miracles, visions, or portals opening to heaven; experiencing an apostle-Paul-like trip to the third heavens (see 2 Corinthians 12:2); or getting a glimpse of some future event. I mean, here I was sacrificing a week of my busy schedule so I could travel hundreds of miles to spend a week in silence at a place so remote that I could not even get a signal on my cell phone, let alone be able to activate my hotspot to the Internet. You would think that would have been good enough for at least an angelic visit to give me some direction in my ministry! I had even been foolish enough to ask God to cause my ministry to go in a specific direction that I so desired. Well, all that seems so mundane now after my week of silence.

What God did reveal to me during this time was my heart's desire. I just had not realized my heart's true desire when I first arrived at the abbey. I thought I knew it, but, in silence, I discovered I really did not understand my own heart. Christians often take Psalm 37:4—*"Delight thyself also in the LORD: and he shall give thee the desires of thine heart"*—quite literally. They spend a lot of time trying to delight themselves in the Lord, hoping that if they get enough *delight*, God will see fit to grant their heart's desire, which they believe to be a healing, a financial miracle, a restored marriage, or something similar. Yet not until the veil is ripped from our hearts do we actually know and understand what our true heart's desire is. Some find that veil ripped from their hearts through a season of prayer, Bible study, or fasting. For me, it was silence.

On that first day here, I had been convinced that I was asking for something that came from the very heart of God. Now, I realize what His heart is asking for, so I tell Him the thing I want most is for Him to have my heart and to find whatever pleasure He can with it. I told Him that in return, I wanted Him to continue hugging me and allowing me to enter into a *devek*.

During this week of silence, my heart has seen what my eyes could not see, my heart has heard what my ears could not hear, and my heart has spoken what my lips could not speak. In silence, I was able to enter that special room in God's heart, that quiet room, that weeping room. In this room, in the same manner I expressed earlier, I found Jesus holding a heart in His hands, a heart that had been broken, and He was weeping over it. He was feeling the heart's hurt and loneliness. He longed to heal the wound that had torn it apart, but the heart's owner would not seek His comfort.

He picked up another heart that was cold and barren, and I watched His tears fall and roll off it. I could sense Him wishing that each tear would somehow penetrate that heart, but the heart's owner would not open it to Him to allow His tears to enter and soften it. As He picked up still another broken heart, I reached out to Him and touched one of His nail-pierced hands. Instantly, I felt His sorrow and pain, as well as the anguish felt by the heart's owner, and all three of us wept.

It was in this quiet, weeping room that I saw clearly my own heart's desire. It was not to have a flourishing ministry, to see more books published, or even to experience a healing of my body. Whatever time I have left here on earth, I only want to be allowed to enter Jesus's quiet room, His weeping room, and be permitted to see the hearts He is holding in His hands, those hearts that He weeps over. I want to weep with Him, and if it is at all possible, I want to find these hearts' owners and let them know that there is a Savior weeping for them who wishes to build a chet, or a bridge, between their broken hearts and His heart of healing. He longs to enter their wounded hearts so that His tears and His nailed-pierced hands can heal those wounds.

May you, also, be stirred to spend time in silence, for it is in silence that you will hear the world's weeping, and God weeping for it. It is in silence that you will perceive His desire to bring peace and healing to wounded and broken hearts. It is in silence where your heart's desire will be transformed to want to reach out to others with His deep and compassionate love.

PART TWO
LESSONS FROM CREATION

PROLOGUE:
LEARNING FROM GOD'S MASTER TEACHERS

*"But ask now the beasts, and they shall teach thee; and the fowls of
the air, and they shall tell thee: or speak to the earth, and it shall teach
thee: and the fishes of the sea shall declare unto thee."*
—Job 12:7–8

"I went to the woods because I wished to live deliberately,
to front only the essential facts of life, and see if I could not
learn what it had to teach, and not, when I came to die,
discover that I had not lived."
—Henry David Thoreau, *Walden*

Of late, I have been feeling very unsettled spiritually. Ever since I entered the sixth decade of my life, I have started to become more and more aware of my mortality. I have walked with God practically all my life, even celebrated my fiftieth spiritual birthday last year during my silent retreat at the abbey. I accepted Jesus as my personal Savior at the age of twelve, and I have grown to love Him more and more. He has been my dearest Friend down through the years, and my hunger and thirst to know Him and grow closer to Him only becomes more intense as I continue to learn about Him and draw nearer to that day when I will see Him face-to-face.

Yes, one day I will leave this world, and I will have the fullness of knowledge about God. (See 1 Corinthians 13:12.) Yet while I remain on earth, I am profoundly aware that there are things I can experience only in this world that I will never experience in eternity. In Psalm 6:5, David says, *"For in death there is no remembrance of thee: in the grave who shall give thee thanks?"* The Hebrew word for *"give…thanks"* in this verse is *yadah*, which, in its Semitic origin, has the idea of shooting an arrow. Additionally, tracing this word through its Canaanite origin, I find that it is speaking about the result of an act. Therefore, this verse refers to praising God following a certain action of His. In this context, I think David is saying that once he has entered eternity, there will be no need to call upon the Lord for deliverance, and there will be no need for God to rescue him from a terrifying situation, because he will be in eternal peace with God.

Likewise, in heaven, we will never find ourselves praising God for a recent healing, because we will never be sick. We will never praise God for a financial miracle, because we will have no need of finances. We will never have to praise the Lord in the midst of suffering or pain, because we will not have to endure suffering or pain. We will never know the gentle, loving touch of God as He heals our broken heart, because we will never experience a broken heart. The Lord has promised to wipe away all tears. (See Revelation 7:17; 21:4.)

Yet there is a special joy in facing a difficult situation and experiencing God's deliverance, a special joy in giving thanks to God for rescuing us. Our singular opportunity to know the particular joy of having Him wipe away our tears, of praising Him in the midst of trial—a joy that not even the angels can know—is while we are living in this physical realm. This present life affords us the ability to experience something new with God that we can have only during our sojourn here.

It is said that the angels do not know the joy of redemption because they do not need to be redeemed. But I will never forget that special joy I experienced when I was only twelve years old, and felt the cleansing forgiveness of Jesus's blood as I received His gift of redemption. I remember dancing around and singing that old hymn, "There's a new name written down in glory, and it's mine."[5] Although there will be untold joys in eternity, where in heaven will we experience a joy like that? Thus, every day that we walk this earth, we are given an opportunity that we will never have

5. C. Austin Miles, "A New Name in Glory," 1910.

in eternity, an occasion to call upon God in the midst of a trial, a disappointment, or a heartbreak, and to know the comfort of His presence and strength.

A second way we can experience God in a special way right now on earth is through the present creation. All around us, God's creation is continually speaking of Him—do you not hear its calls? David heard them. He expressed, *"Let the rivers clap their hands, let the mountains sing together for joy"* (Psalm 98:8 NIV). I have sat through hundreds, probably thousands, of sermons and teachings throughout my life. I have attended Bible college and seminary; I have earned advanced degrees in biblical studies and biblical languages. Yet, I hunger, I long, I groan, to know and experience God in ways that are deeper, richer, fuller. I want to use every moment while I am here on earth to discover something fresh and exciting about my Lord. I have found that He is a well that never runs dry, that I have not even begun to explore the deep and beautiful caverns of His heart.

Accordingly, even as I reflect upon the lessons of the many great teachers I have learned from throughout my life, I know that there are certain teachers in this world that I have not fully been tutored under. That is the reason why, for my second silent retreat, I chose to go to the woods, in the mountains of the Catskills of New York State, to draw close to God. I wanted an opportunity to sit under God's "master teachers" in creation— the living creatures that roam this earth, the birds of the air, and the earth itself, including the mountains, the hills, the valleys, and the streams. Their tuition is free, and their degree is accredited by God Himself. And it is a teaching we can receive only while we are in this world.

I desired to live in the midst of God's creation and exclaim to it, "Tell me of the beauty and majesty of your Creator; teach me as no man or woman has ever taught me; show me your secrets. I will allow the ears of my heart to hear what my physical ears cannot hear; I will allow the eyes of my heart to see what my physical eyes cannot see; and I will allow the lips of my heart to speak praise to our Creator what my physical lips cannot speak. I go to you to 'learn what you have to teach, and not, when I come to die, discover that I have not learned to live.'"

So join me in this new chapter of my journey to the heart of God in silence as I share with you what I learned from the teachers of this "prophetic" conference in the Catskill Mountains. I woke up to the song of the mountains as they sang their praise to God. I visited the streams that run through the Catskills and listened to them clap their hands in praise to our Creator. Perhaps, as we explore these experiences together, we will be like Washington Irving's character Rip Van Winkle, who was awakened from a twenty-year sleep in the Catskills to discover that his whole life, his whole world, had changed. In our case, may we be *transformed into* [Christ's] *image with ever-increasing glory"* (2 Corinthians 3:18 NIV) as we see the glory of God.

In part two, I share many of the words from the journal I kept while I wandered through the Catskills. As I wrote earlier, I haven't included all that is in that journal, for it was written when my heart was joined with the heart of God, and some of the joy and tears seemed too personal to share. Yet whatever I don't share of these joys and tears in this book, I know I will share with you one day because, most likely, after you arrive in heaven, you will wander to a park where there will be a crowd of angels listening as I relate what the master instructors of God's creation taught to this humble work of God while he was still in the flesh.

23

YOU ARE NEVER LOST

"Are not two sparrows sold for a farthing? and one of them shall not fall on the ground without your Father."
—Matthew 10:29

"Not a sparrow falls to the ground without His seeing it."
"But it falls, just the same. What good is seeing it fall?"
—Mark Twain, "The Mysterious Stranger"

There were a lot of twists and turns on the road, but "Old Madge" got me to my destination. Madge is the name my study partner in Chicago gave to my GPS. At times, I cannot figure out what Old Madge is up to. Still, if she says to go left, I go left. And, lo and behold, by putting my trust in Madge, I arrived at my little cabin in the Catskill Mountains—all alone, just God and me once more. This is what is called a writer's cabin, and although I have a manuscript due in January, writing is not my primary purpose for being here. I am beginning my silent retreat, where God is going to show off! And He sure started this adventure with a bang, just to remind me of my purpose for being here.

I had arrived at the cabin earlier today with my car's gas tank almost on empty. So I figured that before I did anything else, I needed to get some gas to feed the car, and pick up some supplies for the week to feed myself. I pulled out old faithful Madge, hit "points of interest," and typed in "gas." Turns out the closest gas station was ten miles away! I looked at Madge and then at my gas gauge, and I figured it was going to be a close one.

Madge commanded me to go left, so I headed off to my left. Even though something told me to go right, I ignored that still, small voice. I turned where Madge told me to turn, turned around when Madge told me to turn around, and made a sharp right when Madge told me to make a sharp right. The next thing I knew, I was driving down a dirt road. I began to wonder just why a gas station would be located off a dirt road. However, just as Sparky the Wonder Dog, my neighbor's pet pit bull, obeys his owner's every command, I continued down the dirt road until it ended at a cliff overlooking a beautiful display of God's creation. Madge was still calmly instructing me to proceed another quarter mile and make a right turn. Looking out over the ravine, I figured that would put me right smack in the creek that I could barely make out, way down below.

I looked nervously at my gas tank and realized I had no idea where there was a gas station or how I was going to locate one. Madge appeared to have really lost it, because she was directing me to another dirt road. I assumed Madge's satellite had been hit by some sunspot that knocked her crazy, so I chose to ignore her and head back to the main road. I figured if I just kept going down that road, I was bound to find a gas station. All the while, I sensed God pointing out His creation to me, wanting me to enjoy each little mountain view and stream, but I was just too worried about running out of gas to enjoy anything at that point, especially paying attention to and admiring God's little gifts. The road I was on seemed endless, with no towns or gas stations in sight. On top of that, I felt totally lost. Even if I came upon a gas station in time, I had no idea how I was going to find my way back to the cabin.

Suddenly, my attention was diverted to the forest of trees that stretched ahead of me as far as the eye could see. I was surprised to find that the leaves had started to turn color. On my way up here, I had been concerned that I would be too early to see the leaves change, because it is only late September, but I will actually be able to see the beginnings of the fall colors. I began to reflect on how each leaf, when green, has just one job to perform, and that is to turn carbon dioxide into oxygen so we can breathe and live. That little green leaf's sole job is to carry out that one function, which is vital to sustaining our lives. When the leaf has finished its job, it dies, after just a few months of life. If I were to pluck it from the tree prematurely, it would turn brown and die; but when it is left on the tree to die its natural death, completing its life cycle, it gives us one last gift—it turns into a glorious display of color, reminding us of the beauty of our Creator.

I began to think about a time almost four years earlier when I had suffered a serious affliction and come close to passing from this life. At the time, I did not care that I was near death, and I was almost disappointed that I survived. Yet I told God that if He did keep me alive, then whatever time He gave me, I would use for His sake. As I saw the glorious colors beginning to appear on the branches of the trees, I felt God was telling me that if I had left this life four years previously, I would merely have turned into a brown leaf, but because He has kept me here for the time He has planned for me to stay, when I do pass from this earth, I will leave behind something that will show the glory and beauty of God.

About that time, I snapped out of my meditation and thought, *I am almost out of gas, and there is no—*. Then I looked up, and there was a little service station, complete with gas pumps. Not only that, but there was a sign indicating that the little town where my cabin was located was just five miles down the road from where the station stood. Had I made a right turn rather than a left turn (against the wishes of Old Madge), I would not have gone thirty miles out of my way. But then again, I would have started my week of silence without God's first lesson for me, and that was to remind me that I am on this earth for only as long as He wishes, and if I stay around for the duration, He will allow me to leave behind something that declares His glory and beauty.

God knew Old Madge would fail me, just as He knows when every sparrow falls. (See Matthew 10:29.) Even though I was trusting in Madge with all my heart and leaning not on my own understanding, even though in all my ways I was acknowledging Madge, she *failed* to direct my paths. (Compare Proverbs 3:5–6.) Interestingly, the first-century equivalent of GPS was a sparrow. Sparrows have homing instincts, and when someone planned a long journey away from home, they would purchase some little sparrows to take with them. Then, when the pilgrim began their journey home, they would release the sparrow and follow it home. Unfortunately, sparrows are very fragile birds and would sometimes die in flight. The poor traveler would then be faced with a moment like I faced when Madge had her nervous breakdown. However, God was reminding me that He is aware of even our loss of direction, whether from the fall of a sparrow or a sunspot disrupting our GPS. Yet He will never fail us; He will intervene and continue to guide us.

I travel back to my little cabin now to begin this journey into the heart of God—to explore His beauty and majesty, and perhaps, like Moses, to see His glory so that I might *know Him*. One Hebrew word for knowing is *yada*, which means to know so intimately that you are willing to share your secrets. During this coming week, in such a *yada*, perhaps God will share His secrets with me.

24

FIVE SMOOTH STONES

"And [David] took his staff in his hand, and chose him five smooth
stones out of the brook, and put them in a shepherd's bag which he
had, even in a scrip; and his sling was in his hand:
and he drew near to the Philistine."
—1 Samuel 17:40

This morning, I awoke to a perfect fall day, so God and I took a drive through the Catskill Mountains. I knew He wanted to show me something, but even while I viewed the beautiful mountains and the lush trees with their many colors, I was not getting any real sense of, *This is it.* Not until we stopped by a little stream. When I got out of the car and began walking along the banks of this stream, I noticed that the streambed was strewn with rocks and stones. Suddenly, the presence of God felt especially close, and I knew this was what He wanted to show me.

I reflected on the fact that, especially in ancient times, wars have been fought over the boundary rights to streams similar to this one, because water was so scarce and precious. I thought particularly of David's battle with Goliath and how the Israelites' war with the Philistines might have erupted over water rights to a strategic stream. Perhaps David had gone to that very disputed brook to pick out the five smooth stones with which he could do battle with the enemy. You get the impression from this passage of Scripture that the stream was near where the battle was taking place.

As I looked down at the stream in the Catskills, I noticed how smooth the stones were. For all I know, those stones could have been there for hundreds of years. The colonials might even have used them as step-ping-stones to cross the stream. I observed the gentle flow of the water and pondered the idea that, year after year, water had continually poured over those stones—sometimes calm waters, as they now were, but other times rough waters as a result of storms or the runoff of melting snow coming down from the heights. It was this constant flow over the years that had worn all the rough edges off the stones.

The presence of God grew stronger as I continued to meditate on these thoughts, and I realized that God had brought me to this little stream to explain something more to me. After I got back to my cabin, I began to examine 1 Samuel 17:40, which describes David picking up the five smooth stones.

People often wonder why David chose five stones. Some say Goliath had four brothers and that David used one stone against each of them. I think that interpretation reads too much into the story, because there is no indication of five brothers taking on David. Instead, I believe that what we find here is a play on words. All eyes were on David when he went to the stream and picked up the stones. He probably held them up and de-clared to everyone, "*Chamesh*," which in Hebrew means "five" but in the Canaanite language means "an army." So David might have been declaring that he was going against the Philistine army with an army of stones.

But perhaps he meant even more than that. He might have declared, "*Chaeshah chalaqi 'avanim.*" This phrase means "five smooth stones," but it could also be a play on the Semitic roots of these words, rendering the meaning "an army of hardened hearts mocking." In other words, David was going to destroy an army that dared to mock the living God. And he would do it with mere stones. (See 1 Samuel 17:26, 45–47.) Personally, I believe that David, who announced to Goliath that he came against him in the name of the Lord, called upon the name of God somewhere in this story, and that this did more to bring down the giant than just one smooth stone. At least, that works for me when I face a giant in my life!

As David picked up those smooth stones from the stream, pondering what he was about to do, perhaps he thought about how, during the times in his life when he fought a bear or a lion through the power of God in order to protect his father's sheep, he had been developing the strong faith he now possessed. Maybe he considered all his days as a shepherd boy, when he walked with God through the calm and through the storms, facing the various dangers that shepherds encountered in those times—from the natural elements in a desert land, to the predatory animals, to the bandits who would try to steal his family's property—and he began to realize that these experiences had been smoothing the rough edges of his growing faith, preparing him for this very day, when he would face a giant in order to save his nation.

All of us have experienced life's "waters" flowing over us, including the rough waters of emotional, physical, and spiritual storms, and these may have been used by God to smooth out the rough edges of our own faith. Perhaps this continual flow has been preparing us for the days when we, too, will be able to raise up a *chamesh*, or an army of faith, to fight against the various giants that will come into our lives to challenge us.

I meditated on this idea, thinking about all the storms I had gone through in my life and how God had come to protect and deliver me each time. The more I realized how the protecting hand of God had been on me through the years, the more I began to weep in overwhelming praise and thanksgiving to Him. I felt like I was in a cloud of glory. It was as though I had fallen into the arms of God and received a big *devek*, or hug, from Him. In response, I clung to Him, never wanting to let Him go. He stroked my heart with His hand, and I felt my heart's rough edges being smoothed away. It was as if He was uncovering the faith that had been buried beneath all the roughness that had developed there. I remembered the years of pain and heartbreak that had caused those rough edges to form, realizing now that God had always been there, that He had never left me or abandoned me. As I wept in His arms, He quietly whispered to me in assurance, "It's all right, I will never leave you, and I will never forsake you." (See Hebrews 13:5.)

I thought again of those stones in the stream and how they remained firmly in place, year after year, through calm weather and storms, becoming smoother and smoother. Over the years, the Lord has been removing all the rough edges of my life in order to uncover a faith that not only was strong and steady, but was also vulnerable enough to feel the gentle flow of the Spirit of God as it now passed over me, wave after wave. I kept clinging to the God whom I have learned to love, and I wept until it seemed as if there were no more tears left. He wept with me, saying over and over, "It's been a long time. Welcome home."

Finally, I just rested in His arms, and I felt as if He were saying, "Now that you have shared your heart with Me, I shall share My heart with you." As He began to reveal to me the secrets of His heart, I started to feel again His pain, suffering, and heartbreak over a lost world. His sorrow over believers who seek God only to satisfy their own desires, never considering that He has desires, as well, that He has a heart that longs to be loved in return.

While God shared the secrets of His heart, we wept together, and I renewed a promise I had made to Him during my first silent retreat, at the Abbey of Gethsemani—that if He would let me weep on His shoulder when my heart was broken, I would let Him weep on my shoulder when His heart was broken. And this time, I ended with a prayer: "Dear Father God of my heart, let me not leave this world until I have experienced just a small token of how great Your love is—a love that is more powerful than the Catskill mountains and more beautiful than their valleys."

Including a valley with a certain stream containing solid, smooth stones.

25

IN THE COOL OF THE DAY

"And they heard the voice of the LORD God walking in the garden in the cool of the day: and Adam and his wife hid themselves from the presence of the LORD God amongst the trees of the garden."
—Genesis 3:8

Earlier this morning, I was sitting in my cabin in the Catskills when I decided to step outside. The sun had just risen, and there was a gentle, cool breeze. I heard the birds chirping their morning song, and everything was so pleasant, I experienced a sense of peace and joy.

That is why, when I read the above verse, I felt that somehow, in that tense and dramatic moment in the garden of Eden, the words *"in the cool of the day"* seemed woefully out of place. Or maybe I am just being influenced by the Academy Award-winning song by Hoagy Carmichael and Johnny Mercer entitled "In the Cool, Cool, Cool of the Evening." The song is joyful and happy, and we usually associate "the cool of the day" with something pleasurable. Yet in Genesis 3:8, the phrase is thrown into the midst of something shameful, dreadful, and sad. Any book editor worth his salt would scratch that phrase right out of the passage—yet there it is as part of God's Word. I happen to believe that every word and every phrase in Scripture has meaning and purpose. God did not throw that phrase in there to create some poetic mood; it is there to convey to us a deeper understanding of the situation.

We should note that the first part of the verse says that Adam and Eve *"heard"* the voice of God. The Hebrew word translated *"heard"* is *shama',* which means more than just hearing something; it is hearing with under-standing, attention, and/or a response. Sometimes the word *shama'* is used in a judicial sense. For example, we say that a judge will *hear* a case. The judge is not just listening to the legal arguments casually but is listening with intent, paying close attention to every detail in order to make a just de-cision or ruling. If the word for *"heard"* were used in a piel (intensive) form, it would mean to summon or call—like my neighbor calling for Sparky to stop barking at me. But it is not used here in a piel form; it is in a simple qal (active) form. That means when Adam and Eve initially heard God's voice, He was not calling to them to come out of hiding, because they hid only after they heard His voice in the garden. (See Genesis 3:8, 10.) This makes sense, because God was not playing a game of hide-and-seek with Adam and Eve. He certainly knew where they were, and Adam and Eve were fully aware that He knew where they were.

Then, in Genesis 3:9, after they hid themselves, God called to Adam, asking, *"Where are you?"* (NKJV). The Hebrew word rendered *"Where are you?"* is simply the word *'oy.* You might be familiar with the Yiddish expres-sion *"Oy vey,"* which is loosely interpreted as "Oh, woe." It is generally be-lieved that *oy* in the Yiddish phrase is derived from the German or Dutch *au,* which means "ouch" or "oh." Yet there are many orthodox rabbis who believe this expression stems from Biblical Hebrew and was a common expression in Semitic languages. In fact, in Aramaic, the word *oy* means "how." It is also a common term in Hebrew used to express the idea of how, where, when, who, and other such words.

What I find interesting is that within the Semitic culture, *'oy* is some-times used for the idiomatic expression "Where is he?" That is most likely why translators render this word in Genesis 3:8 as *"Where are you?"* But this idiomatic Semitic expression is actually rhetorical, meaning, "Where are you? You are nowhere." In other words, if we render *'oy* to reflect this particular expression, then what God is really saying is, "Adam, you are nowhere." If the orthodox Jews are right about the origin of the word *'oy,* then the voice of God calling in the garden was a lament; He was saying, "Woe is Me. Where are you, Adam? For you are nowhere in My heart."

Let's now return to the concept of *"cool"* in Genesis 3:8. Indeed, God was walking through His garden on earth *"in the cool of the day."* The

Hebrew word translated *"cool"* is *ruach*, which is the word for a spirit. It is also used for a wind, the mind, or an emotion. The word for *"day"* is simply *yom*, which could mean a twenty-four-hour day, but could also refer to a year, a period of time, or even a moment of time. Perhaps God was walking in the garden to capture the emotion of the moment. He wanted to experience the joy of being loved. But because of Adam and Eve's sin, He could not experience His love for them being returned.

Of course, God does not have physical legs on which He walks. The Hebrew word translated *"walking"* is *halak*, which can be used literally or figuratively. There are a variety of applications for this word. For example, *halak* can also refer to a manner of life. Indeed, the word *halaka*, which denotes a righteous walk, is derived from it. In its Semitic root, *halak* has the idea of going or moving as opposed to just sitting. I like to look at it that way, and I will tell you why.

This morning, as I was about to set out to drive through the Catskills, I realized I first had to shave and clean up the cabin. Yet I felt as if God was already in the car waiting for our drive through the mountains, and that He was calling out, "Come on, let's get started! You can shave later. I am the only one who will see you, and I don't care if you have a beard or not. Let's move *in the cool of the day.*" Or, "Let's capture and enjoy the moment of this emotional experience." Or, "Let's enjoy the move of My Spirit in this moment." I shout back and say, "Oh, but I have to write up this word study first; I have to clean up the cabin a little, I have to…." And God is saying, "*Oy.*" In other words, "Where are you? You have let the cares of this world remove you from My heart. What are you doing that is more important than our time together? What you are doing can wait."

I picture the same type of scenario in the garden of Eden. God was ready to move forward and enjoy the moment with Adam and Eve, but because of their sin, they could not face Him; they could not enjoy that moment with Him. And God began to lament.

Thus, I believe the words *"in the cool of the day"* were included in this narrative to tell us that God is always ready to enjoy a moment, to enjoy the move of His Spirit, with us. But sometimes we cling to some sin and avoid Him, or we are too preoccupied with the cares of this world to join with Him in that moment. He is ready to forgive our sin; He is certainly willing to overlook a four-day-old beard. He only wants us to spend a moment in the Spirit with Him. And if we find something more important than spending that moment with Him to enjoy the gentle breeze of His Spirit while it is still blowing, we may miss a real blessing, because the Spirit moves only when He wants to—not when we are ready or want Him to move. As John 3:8 says, *"The wind blows where it wishes, and you hear the sound of it, but cannot tell where it comes from and where it goes. So is everyone who is born of the Spirit"* (NKJV).

Too often, we try to regulate God or program Him to move during one hour on Sunday morning during the worship service—when *we* are ready for Him. We go to church and say, "Okay, Lord, this is it; this is the time we want You to move, so move now, fill us now with Your presence." There are so many other times during the week when God is ready to move, but we are just too busy, too wrapped up in the pursuits of life, to walk with Him *in the cool of the day*. God simply says to us, "'Oy, why are we intimate only when you are ready?" What if, some Sunday morning, we were ready to worship God, but He were to say, "'Oy, I was ready last night, but you were not. Today I have a 'headache'; you go and enjoy your music and have fun, but the moment has passed for Me"? When the breeze of the Spirit is blowing, it is best that we do not have some sin holding us back, or some other activity occupying us, lest we miss a special and precious moment with God.

By the way, I need to end this little study now because God is in my car right now honking the horn, and if I don't close this out, He will leave without me!

26

MOUNTAINS AND STREAMS

"Let the floods clap their hands: let the hills be joyful together."
—Psalm 98:8

Many people come to the mountains in order to fish in the streams, while others come to hunt. Still others come in the wintertime to ski. I have little interest in fishing, I do not hunt, and I am getting a little too old to ski. I come to the mountains for something even greater—to learn of the beauty, strength, and faithfulness of God.

I have been reading from Psalm 98:8 in my Hebrew Bible. The word translated *"floods"* in the King James Version is *naharot*, which comes from the root word *nahar*, which means a stream or a river. This morning, God and I parked the car by a parking area near a stream that runs along Highway 23A. It appears that this stream flows right from the mountain in the heart of the Catskills. I closed my Hebrew Bible for a moment, and God and I just sat and listened to the water running downstream. As the water moved over the many rocks, it really did sound like it was clapping its hands, just as David describes in the above verse. It was like a joyful, appreciative clapping of hands after a great performance. The sun was beating down on those rocks, and the water passed over them as if it was intended to be their constant cooling companion.

Of course, right behind the stream stood the great Catskill Mountains. The word translated *"hills"* in Psalm 98:8 is *harim*, which is the word for a mountain or a range of hills. The Catskills are a range of mountains, and if you listen closely—that is, if you listen with your heart—you will hear them rejoice together. The Hebrew word translated *"be joyful"* is *ranan*, which my lexicon tells me is "a ringing cry of joy." But this word means more than just a ringing cry of joy. If we go back to its Canaanite roots, the original word was used to describe Bedouins who sat around a campfire at night singing a joyful song without any instruments. *Ranan* has also has been used to express a melodious sound or a series of sounds that are in harmony with each other. In the context of this verse, the harmony is with God. Additionally, the word *sing* is often associated with *ranan*. You might say it applies to an a cappella choral group. As I close my eyes and begin to listen with my heart, I can almost hear the streams and mountains singing together in a beautiful a cappella chorus. I picture God standing up and waving His arms toward them, as if leading a great orchestra or directing a large choir singing a joyful song.

In looking closely at this passage, I have discovered something I have never noticed before in my forty years of studying Classical Hebrew. The root word for stream (*nahar*) is spelled just like the root word for mountain (*har*), only the Hebrew letter nun is added to the beginning of the word. The word for *mountain* is spelled hei, resh, while the word for stream is spelled nun, hei, resh. These two words are apparently closely related.

The very spelling of the word *har* cries out to be noticed, to gain our attention and cause us to listen to that still, small voice from God. The hei carries the meaning of *hinayni*, which means "Here I am," while the resh urges us to move forward. Thus, *har* (mountain) is whispering this message from God: "I am as formidable as this mountain. I will always be there, and I have your back, so don't be afraid to move forward." The word *nahar* has the same message, only with a nun in front of it. That nun encourages us to break down walls of separation, to not let anything stop us when God tells us to move forward.

This stream that I am sitting beside appears to be gently flowing from the mountain, just moving forward. I feel as if it is telling me that it is like the stream of my life, which flows from the mountain of God, and all I need to do is wade into it, sit back, and enjoy this ride through life. In fact, the letter nun also signifies "fish." A fish just flows along with the currents of the streams it travels, feeding, relaxing, and enjoying the ride. So again, if my life springs from the mountain of God, I can flow with the stream of life—feeding, relaxing, and finding pleasure in the ride. Regardless of the obstacles, I can just keep moving with the flow of God, never needing to worry because, like a great mountain, God is my strength.

While enjoying the singing of the mountains and the clapping hands of the stream, I heard them tell me to be sure to pay attention to that still, small voice of God, and when He tells me to move forward, I should just flow with His life-stream, not letting any obstacle stand in my way, knowing that I am flowing from a Great Mountain whom no one can challenge, and who has my back.

Many mountains are snow-covered, and some are just rocky and barren, but the Catskills are covered with trees that are now in full bloom. The leaves are all changing color to create a gloriously colorful blanket that appears soft and comfortable. I told God I would just love to jump in the middle of it and roll around, then slide down this marvelous carpet into the cool stream and ride the rest of the way through life guided by the ebb and flow of the currents. I felt God sort of chuckle and say, "Bingo. Isn't that what I have been trying to get through your stubborn head all these years?"

27

ENJOY THE MOMENT

"O Lord, thou hast deceived me, and I was deceived:
thou art stronger than I, and hast prevailed:
I am in derision daily, every one mocketh me."
—Jeremiah 20:7

Most modern translations of the above verse have Jeremiah say that the Lord *"deceived"* him. Some use the word *"misled,"* while others use *"persuaded," "enticed,"* or *"seduced."* The Hebrew word is *pititani*, which comes from the root word *patah*, which means to allure, to deceive, to entice, to persuade, or to seduce. *Patah* is repeated twice in the passage. In the King James Version, Jeremiah accuses the Lord of *deceiving* him, and then says that he was *deceived*. When a Bible translation chooses a particular word in the first instance, then it will follow with the same word in the second instance.

However, since there is such a wide range of meaning to the word *patah*, there is nothing written in stone that says we should render it with one particular English word or that we must use the same word when it is used later, even if it is in the same sentence. It is really the context that guides us regarding which English word to apply. There is really no reason we could not render this as, for example, "You deceived me, and I was seduced," or "You seduced me, and I was deceived." Either version could be correct, yet they convey something a bit different from one another.

In the Aramaic, the word means to be spacious, open, and abundant. In the Arabic, the word has the idea of someone in the prime of life. And the origin of *patah* does not carry the idea of deception but of simplemind-edness, lacking in judgment.

Perhaps what is going on here is not so much that Jeremiah feels God did a number on him, but that God led him to believe he was something special, one in million, called to do a great work. And the deception came from himself. He started out believing he was going to do it all, but then, when he ended up in prison, he realized that he had deceived himself. He was really no different from anyone else; he wasn't the knight in shining armor that he once thought he was.

The word "*thou*," or "*you*," in "*thou hast deceived me*" is not in the orig-inal Hebrew. It is merely implied. Literally, you would say, "O Lord, I am deceived." Actually, the first time *patah* is used in this verse, it is in a hiphal (causative) form, so that Jeremiah is saying, "O Lord, I was caused to be de-ceived." The second time the word is used, it is in a niphal (reflexive) form. Thus, we could render the sentence as, "O Lord, I was caused to be de-ceived, and I deceived myself." When we examine the Semitic root of this word, therefore, I believe Jeremiah is not really accusing God of deception. Rather, he is saying that in his youthfulness, he was caused to be seduced into believing that he could do great things, but he only deceived himself.

Obviously, Jeremiah's walk with God was much closer than the walk I have with God, and yet I am not for a moment going to think God has ever *deceived* me. However, I have no problem believing that I often *deceive* myself. Sometimes, in my anxiousness to please and serve God, I venture out on "faith," believing God has called me to do something, but then I fall flat on my face. History is littered with the dry, sunbaked bones of Christians who have stepped out on faith and found themselves facedown in the mud. They knew they had a call from God on their lives, but in their own *patah*, or deception, they pursued their mission recklessly, picking up every off-colored stone as a confirmation from God.

I once knew a pastor who had a definite call from God on his life; I could sense and feel it in this man. When I would pray with him, it seemed like the heavens opened. He had a genuine love for God and prayerfully considered every decision he made. He believed God had called him to de-velop a retreat center where world-renowned Christian leaders would come and hold conferences. This retreat center would have a large auditorium, conference rooms, classrooms, a dining room, and a beautiful campus. The center would also house a Christian school and eventually a Bible college.

Prophets from all over came and prophesied over him that he would receive three million dollars to build this retreat center, and he began to build his staff and seek funding. The funds started to come in, and when this pastor saw an old high-rise building go on the market, he jumped at the chance to purchase it. The building really was not suited at all for what God had called him to do, but he figured in faith that God would work that out. He didn't yet have enough money to cover the purchase of the building, so he secured a heavy mortgage to obtain it. At the rate the funds were coming in, he could have had the entire three million in about three years, and he never would have had to take out any mortgage. But then that high-rise would have sold, and he would have lost his chance for a great opportunity to fulfill God's call on his life. This was, after all, God's work, and he was called to it; the sooner he got this retreat center up and running, the better.

Eventually, the high-rise proved to be a money pit, as well as totally inadequate for a conference center. In a couple of years, he and his church were forced into bankruptcy, and the bank foreclosed on the building. The pastor resigned from his position at the church and moved away. I heard that two years later, God took him home. About the same time, a major corporation that had built a beautiful corporate office building—equipped with an auditorium, conference rooms, classrooms, and a beautiful ten-acre campus—went bankrupt and was forced to sell the property, which was located just a couple of miles away from that pastor's former church. The price was three million dollars.

God did not *patah*, or deceive, that pastor. The call was real, and God had a wonderful plan in mind. But this pastor allowed his calling to deceive him; he deceived himself and jumped ahead of God. Had he waited for God's timing and not his own, he would have carried out God's plan for a beautiful conference center.

Perhaps this is why God has called me to the Catskills—to prevent me from making the same mistake Jeremiah and my pastor friend made.

Like other Christians, I feel a sense of calling, a purpose. But we can begin to deceive ourselves as we try to bring about our calling in our own way and in our own time. Jeremiah's experience reminds me that such a move could put me right into a pit. You see, because I am getting older, I feel like there is not much time left for me to fulfill my calling. I feel I must jump in there and get things moving. That is why, as I drive through the Catskills, relaxing and not thinking about any calling, I start feeling a sense of anxiousness. I start feeling as if I should be doing something to get this calling on the move. Yet God is saying, "Relax, it is My plan, not yours. Don't jump ahead of Me. Let me accomplish it in My own time. Right now, let's just enjoy our time together and not think about the complexities involved in fulfilling My plan."

So I begin another day of my silent retreat here in the Catskills, apparently accomplishing absolutely nothing in fulfilling God's plan for my life, just "wasting" another day. It is just God and I, enjoying the moment, letting Him take care of the future. The only thing that is important is this moment. God and I together—that is all that matters in this world.

28

HEALING FOR A SICK HEART

"The heart is deceitful above all things,
and desperately wicked: who can know it?"
—Jeremiah 17:9

Jeremiah really seemed to love that word *deceitful*, didn't he? Here it is again, in an earlier passage. However, unlike in Jeremiah 20:7, where he used the word *patah*, which is rendered as "*deceived*" in many translations but has more of the idea of being seduced or persuaded, this time, the word that is rendered in English as "*deceitful*" is *'aqob*. Maybe it is not so much Jeremiah who likes that word *deceit* as it is the translators. Nonetheless, here I am once again looking at that word. When I started my journey into silence in the Catskills, I asked the Lord for a word to describe this special time of silence, and what word do I get? *Deceit*.

God and I went off on another journey into the mountains this morning. As I have done each morning, I asked the Lord, "Where to?" Today, I felt prompted to travel below the mountains so I could look up at them. That is when I realized I had come to the Catskills at the perfect time of year. As I described earlier, the leaves are just beginning to change color. I looked up at the tree-covered mountains, which had the appearance of a lush tapestry of multiple colors. Every tree on the mountain was flush with multicolored leaves, so full and lush it was almost like a bouquet of flowers. The entire foliage was luxuriant and perfect. I commented to God again how His mountain is so full of beauty, so rich, every tree covered in a glorious blanket of leaves.

There is a side road leading up into the mountain, and I sensed that still, small voice guiding me to follow this road. As I drove up the mountain, I became aware of the fact that I was passing right through that rich and perfect garden that I had seen from the base of the mountain. It took me a while to realize this, because things did not seem as beautiful and perfect-looking up close. I was surrounded by dead trees, or trees that were only half-filled with leaves, while their other halves appeared to be dead and lifeless. The ground was covered with decaying and rotting vegetation. The foliage here did not seem as luxuriant as it had from a distance.

I sensed God whispering to me, "That is your heart." I had to pull to the side of the road because I began to weep. I understood why God had taken me out this morning to the base of the mountain and then up into its interior. When God sees my heart, He sees a lot of dead wood, scattered ruins, decay, and rot that are masked to the outside world, just as the tops of the trees with their colorful leaves masked the ugly, dead waste on this mountain. I realized that people look at me from a distance, just as I had looked at the Catskills from below. They read my blog or my books and think I am some sort of guru who has all his spiritual ducks in a row and walks around singing hymns 24/7. They see my heart from a distance and remark, "My, my, what a spiritual giant you are. Oy, you have such a heart for God. Come, come everyone, let us sit under the teachings of this great man of God." Yet God is not looking at my heart from a distance. He is traveling through the interior of my heart, and it does not look so beautiful inside.

As I weep, I feel so ashamed of myself. How dare I demand that God give me some special revelation, a miracle or a sign? How dare I ask anything of God when my heart is filled with such deceit and pride? I just lap up all the positive reviews of my books like a thirsty dog lapping up water from a stream. Do I even dare ask God for something special when I practice little deceits and cover-ups? Oh yes, I pretend to be such an intelligent and knowledgeable person so people will stand in awe of me. Yet, all the while, I fear that one day Toto will pull back the curtain and reveal that the great Hebrew teaching wizard is nothing more than a friendly little guy holding his kingdom together with a lot of bluff and bluster.

How dare I come to the Catskills and tell God, "Well, here I am, spending all my time with You, worshipping You, giving You my full attention, and even sacrificing areas of my life for You. Surely You will say, 'Oy, and such good things you have done for Me. You have certainly earned yourself a miracle or two.'" (I seem to have forgotten what I learned during my last silent retreat.)

I weep before God, confessing that I am just a fraud, a phony, who has no more of the Holy Spirit than an uneducated country preacher who just preaches from his heart.

I look further at that word for "*deceitful*," *'aqob*, and find that it comes from a Semitic root meaning a hill, a slippery hill. I recalled walking down a little hill yesterday in order to get to a stream at the base of the mountain. It wasn't until I was sliding down the hill that it dawned on me that the slope was steeper and slipperier than I had anticipated. That little hill is so like my heart. I look at it and see a little cliff, a little sin, a little lie, a little deceit, and think nothing of it. It's okay, no one is getting hurt. In fact, it may even be helpful to others. But it is a slippery slope, and I find myself falling into a deeper sin. The heart is slippery, sly, and insidious; it can easily fool us.

This area of New York certainly has a lot of hills. When I am traveling up a hill, I cannot see what is over the top and on the other side of it. That is so like my heart—so hilly that no one can really see what is on the other side, the side I have hidden from everyone, except for God, and I can tell that He is not too happy about it. How does the King James Version say it? "*The heart is…desperately wicked.*" The Hebrew word translated "*desperately wicked*" is *'anash*. This is not one of the *ra* words that is the usual Hebrew word for expressing "wickedness." *'Anash* means to be sickly, weak, and frail. In this verse, it is used as a passive participle, meaning *woefully sick*. As I looked around at all the dead and dying trees, as well as the rotting, decaying leaves, in this forest, covered by a top layer of the luxuriant foliage of the other trees, I realized that all the compliments and praise I have received from my books and writings have only provided a luxuriant foliage to cover up a sick heart.

I considered how, last night, I sensed God was asking me to pray for a healing, but I kept heroically telling Him, "No, I will not seek this time for self-edification. I am not here to bribe You into healing my infirmities. There are more important things than my health at stake here." Now, however, I realize that God was asking me to pray for the healing of my sick heart. I can live with physical infirmities, but I cannot live with a sick heart. I need God to heal it. I parked my car, walked into the woods, lay down in all that rotting and decaying vegetation, and let God overhaul my engine.

29

UNSPEAKABLE JOY

"For in the resurrection they neither marry, nor are given in marriage, but are as the angels of God in heaven."
—Mathew 22:30

I had lain in the woods in the interior of the Catskill Mountains, having a season of prayer—prayer of repentance. Once again, I began to experience the joy of the cleansing power of the blood of Jesus as He created in me a new heart. As I reflected on the joy of this restoration in my relationship with God, I became aware of another joy, a joy that not many people take advantage of here in this life. I began to breathe in the mountain air and found it so refreshing that I experienced a joy of just living, of just being able to inhale the air that was being oxygenated by God's creation. I never realized the joy in just breathing. The smells around me were like perfume, and when I touched God's creation, I could feel the vibrations of life. I stood up and began to take in the joy of experiencing life and the life around me. Even all the life that had ended, the dampness of the decaying vegetation, still gave off a freshness as it contributed to the beginnings of other new life.

I began to feel a joy so rich and deep that I thought no one else in this world could experience such joy in the presence of God. But, of course, others have and do. Then again, there are those who do not experience a joy of this measure or level. I reflected on how Jesus said that in the resurrection, we will be like the angels, who do not marry. (See, for example, Matthew 22:30.) Jesus spoke those words in Aramaic, and the Aramaic Bible, the Peshitta, uses the word *nasav* for *"marry."* This is a common Semitic word (nsb) found in many of the Semitic languages, particularly in the ancient Akkadian and Persian languages. It is often used in association with the goddess Inanna, or Ishtar, who was the goddess of fertility and sexuality. Jesus is not referring to marriage here in the sense of a wedding ceremony and a couple walking hand in hand through life together. He is not saying that a couple who had been married will no longer share that special spiritual relationship that they shared on earth. They will just not consummate it in a physical sense. If you will forgive me for being so bold, Jesus is really saying in this verse that there will be no sex in heaven. The spiritual and emotional closeness that a couple experiences in their intimacy will continue, but the carnal aspect will no longer play into the matter.

The Talmud teaches that "in the world to come there is neither eating nor drinking, nor the bearing of children, nor commerce, nor envy, nor hatred, nor contention."[6] Thus, we are able to experience pleasures and joys in this natural body that the angels will never experience. In making reference to the angels, Jesus might have been playing on His contemporary audience's knowledge of the book of Enoch, and correcting their perceptions. The book of Enoch was read and studied by the Jews during the time of Jesus. In fact, many believed it was an inspired book. This book taught that some angels desired to experience the physical, lustful, and carnal aspect of a sexual relationship but could not because they had no physical bodies. So they implanted themselves into women, and were actually born into this world in a physical body in which they could experience all the things they could not experience as a spiritual being, such as eating, drinking, and "giving in marriage" (sexual relationships).

I recalled a dream I once had where I felt I was in heaven, only I was on some planet that had two suns (I probably dreamed this because I am a science fiction fan), and I was on the shore of a lake with a team of other believers in heaven. Suddenly, we heard an angelic crowd approaching us, and I could hear their expectant conversations. They were saying, "The saints are here; they are here to tell us their stories." Suddenly, we were surrounded by these angelic beings, who begged us to tell our stories of how Jesus delivered us from our troubles during our earthly sojourn. How Jesus brought joy to us when we had a broken heart. How Jesus came to us

---

6. Babylonian Talmud Beracot 17:1.

and redeemed us from our sins. At that moment, I began to relive all these times here on earth and the joys I had experienced with Jesus in the natural world. I became aware that the angels surrounding me were also vicariously experiencing this joy through me.

In this dream, I realized I was on an eternal mission to visit all the angels in the universe and share this special joy with them. I found myself playing a musical instrument like a piano or keyboard, and I was singing. Yes, I was actually singing. In this natural body, I can clear a room pretty quickly when I start to sing, but in that heavenly state, I was singing in a beautiful voice songs of praise about the great victories and deliverances I had experienced while in the natural world. The angels' rejoicing only became greater as I continued to sing, and my heart cried out, "Oh, God, I wish I could do this for eternity." I heard a voice say, "That you shall." Then I woke up.

Now, here in the Catskill Mountains, I cried out to God, "Yes, the angels cannot experience the joy I am experiencing right now, for it is a joy of being alive in this physical body, and the angels do not have physical bodies. However, one day, they will experience this special type of joy; my mission in heaven will be to allow them to experience this joy through me." No wonder the angels rejoice over the repentance of one sinner. (See Luke 15:10.) That is another believer who will spend eternity sharing with them the memories of their physical joys and of God's deliverances.

As I reflected on all this, I felt God whisper to me, "Leave the Catskills and go fifteen miles outside of town to have lunch. I want to show you something." I did not want to leave this enchanted forest filled with the presence of God, feeling the life all around me, but the prompting to leave was so strong that I made my way to my car.

30

THE JOY OF HOSPITALITY

*"Be not forgetful to entertain strangers: for thereby some have
entertained angels unawares."*
—Hebrew 13:2

"Seek to show hospitality."
—Romans 12:13 (ESV)

s I drove away from the mountains into a little town about fifteen miles
outside the Catskills, I reflected on Hebrews 13:2, the verse about
"entertaining angels unaware." The word in the Greek that is rendered as
"entertain strangers" is *philoxenias*, which is a compound word combining
philos, meaning friend, and *xenos*, meaning strangers. The word has the
idea of being friendly with strangers. It is sometimes used for hospitality.

The Greek word translated *"angels"* is *angelous*, which means messenger and is often used for a supernatural messenger. While the Bible seems
to indicate that angels can take on a physical appearance while delivering
messages from God and helping people in other ways, they are still not
physical beings, but spiritual ones. The Aramaic word for "angel" is *malak*,
which comes from the same root as the word for "king." A king had one primary purpose, and that was to protect the people under him. That is why
a king was so honored and given such respect by his subjects; his people
looked up to him to protect them from foreign invaders, to administer jus-
tice, and to provide for them when they could not provide for themselves.
Such is the role of the angels.

It is interesting that *malak* also has the same root as the word for "salt." Salt is an ancient preservative; it protects meat from spoiling. Again, an angel is one who protects. Additionally, *malak* is a word used for counsel and advice. Another role of angels is to guide us in the right direction, which is often the reason advice is given. Until we are in heaven, we will not really know just how much the angels provided for us while we were here on earth.

I was pondering all this when I walked into a little café in town. I am normally shy about entering this type of restaurant because it seems so much a community place. I would prefer a more impersonal, fast-food type of eatery. However, I realized this is sort of a tourist town, and the residents are probably used to strangers eating in their local café. I noticed how the owner of the establishment had taken much care in its layout and maintenance. It was easy to see they were proud of their café and the work that had gone into it.

Yes, there is a special joy in work and in the accomplishment of work. Perhaps God brought me out of the mountains into the community to see how the people took pride in their little town, keeping it clean and maintaining its buildings so they could show it off to the tourists—not unlike God taking pride in His creation so He could show it off to humanity.

If that was the case, how disappointed the people in this town would be if no one came to admire their work. I found I was indeed welcomed in this little café, not as a regular patron, as they knew I would most likely never return, but it was almost as if they wanted a stranger in there so he could enjoy their handiwork, and take pleasure in the meal they provided and their labors to prepare it.

This little café had a woman's first name in its title, suggesting that it was meant to be just like home: "You all come in, have a bite to eat, and let's just chitchat for a while." As I sat down, I was greeted by my waitress, a young woman of about college age. I noticed that on my right were about three tables pushed together, and there were four women sitting there with their Bibles open.

Since my time in the Catskills had turned into a celebration of just being alive, I decided to really enjoy myself and order a hamburger. I have been told that, at my age, red meat is a type of food I must eliminate from my diet, but on a special occasion such as this, I was sure one homemade burger would not send me prematurely to heaven. After my order arrived, I bit into my hamburger, and it was probably one of the best burgers I have eaten in a long time (actually the only burger I have eaten in a long time). I could tell this was not thrown together like a fast-food burger; this was handcrafted and made with care. Apparently, even the cook in the kitchen took pride in his work to bring some pleasure to strangers.

As I was enjoying my burger, a young man with Semitic features came into the café, sat down, and ordered a cup of coffee. He appeared to be in his thirties and was wearing casual clothes typical of the area. At first, I took him to be one of the locals, but I later learned that, like me, he was a stranger to the community. He looked in my direction and smiled, but he did not say anything. He was welcomed in the café, too, even though his order could add little to the coffers. The employees seemed to be glad he was there just to enjoy the atmosphere they had created. They were indeed showing *philoxenias*, friendliness to strangers, for no other reason than the pure satisfaction of being able to share their pride and joy with them. Even by serving a simple cup of coffee, they were entertaining this man who was a stranger, as I was.

So this was why God brought me out of the Catskill Mountains to this little café. He wanted me to know and realize that just as we humans spend time creating and maintaining our dwellings, decorating them during the holidays, and offering hospitality to bring joy to others, God desires to use His creation, which He maintains, decorates on holidays, and provides to offer hospitality, simply to share His joy with us. How often we overlook the little gifts from God, such as a squirrel that runs up to us and wiggles its nose, or a bird that sings its morning song. We often just ignore these things and go on our busy way, feeling miserable, when all the time, God is filling this world with gifts to ease our burdens.

Our Middle-Eastern-looking friend was just sitting back and enjoying the surroundings, not even drinking his coffee. I began to contemplate angels again, thinking that maybe one day in heaven, I might even explain to angels the glorious taste of a hamburger, and how delicious this burger from the Catskills was, for they do not even know the simple joy of biting into a burger.

I sensed God reminding me that every moment I live in this world in a physical body, I will experience joys that I will spend an eternity sharing. One day, I will indeed entertain angels with every story about the joys that I experienced through Christ Jesus. I must not allow a moment to be wasted; I must not allow a moment to be used for the enemy, because that will be a moment lost for eternity that could have been a great story to tell the angels one day.

31

SURPRISES AT THE CAFÉ

"Blessed be the name of God for ever and ever:
for wisdom and might are his."
—Daniel 2:20

Right after the young Semitic man had walked into the café, another man who was likely in his seventies, and a woman of similar age whom I assumed was his wife, came in and sat down at the table to my left. The man was apparently quite comfortable in this little café, and he called out to the waitress, "Well, no hug for your old grandpa? After my little granddaughter goes off to the big city of New York, I won't be seeing much of her anymore." "Oh, gramps, you know I will be back as often as possible," the waitress said as she gave her grandfather a big hug.

About that time, a middle-aged couple, carrying Bibles, walked into the café and sat down with the women sitting to my right who had their Bibles open. The older man turned his attention away from his granddaughter and called out to the gentleman who had just walked in, "Hey, preacher, nice sermon last Sunday." The preacher said, "Thank you. Do you remember what it was about?" The older man's wife said to him, "Hush, you know you were not in church last Sunday." The preacher, trying to bail the man out of the tough spot that he'd just put himself in, launched into a story about President Calvin Coolidge, who went to church one Sunday while his wife stayed at home. When President Coolidge's wife asked what the minister had preached on, the president replied, "He preached on sin." "Well," his wife responded, "what did he have to say about sin?" "He's against it," said President Coolidge.

This little story seemed to break the ice and draw us all into the conversation, with everyone's attention directed to the older man, who put his arm around his granddaughter's waist and pulled her closer to him. Turning to me and the other quiet gentleman who had come in after I had, he boasted, "My little granddaughter here is off to New York City, where she will take a job with a TV news station and become a foreign correspondent to Israel." The young girl slapped her grandfather on the shoulder and said, "Oh, gramps, it is just an internship, and this correspondence stuff is just a dream."

Since this seemed to be a community affair, I figured it was time to join in on the conversation, and I said, "Well, internships usually turn into full-time jobs." Then the older man noticed my baseball cap, which reads, "Chaim Bentorah Hebrew Teacher." He said to his granddaughter, "Well, lookie here. We have a Hebrew teacher. Maybe he can give you a few lessons. Say something in Hebrew, Cheeim." I sort of choked and looked at the young Semitic man in front of me, who suddenly said, "How about *baruch hashem*?" The man spoke those words in flawless Hebrew. I was surprised, and so was the grandfather, whose eyes lit up. He turned to the preacher and said, "Hey, preacher, lookie here. We have two of God's special people in the café. I know you preached about them; the wife told me about your sermon and the Jews going back to Israel and all that." The pastor corrected the man, saying, "They are God's chosen people, not special people." The young stranger then added, "Your pastor is right; we are all special in God's eyes. The Jewish people have just been chosen to lead others to an understanding of God. Jesus Himself was Jewish, you know."

"So, who is this Barrack Shem fellow?" the older man inquired. I jumped in and said, "*Baruch hashem*. It means 'Blessed be the Name.' By the way, I am not Jewish. I am just a retired Hebrew instructor, but our friend here must be Jewish because his Hebrew is flawless, like a rabbi's." The older man asked, "You a rabbi?" The Semitic man only smiled and nodded.

"We are just about to start our weekly Bible study," the pastor said. "You are welcome to join us." I responded that I needed to continue my journey, and our rabbi friend said that he also had to go, but he thanked the pastor for his invitation.

The pastor then asked the rabbi if he would say a blessing for the young waitress before she went off to her new job, and if he would offer a blessing over their Bible study before he left. The rabbi closed his eyes and said, "*Baruch ata Adonai Eloheinu, melech ha'olam, hagomel lahayavim tovot.*" This is translated, "Blessed are You, Lord our God, King of the Universe, who bestows good things upon the unworthy."

As the young man and I stood to pay our bills, the older man said to the rabbi, "Well, my wife here says that because Israel is a nation again, that is fulfilling some sort of prophecy. That's what you preached about, wasn't it, preacher? The wife told me the whole sermon. She said Jesus is going to return very soon, yep, that is what you said, all right. How about you, rabbi, think Jesus is going to return soon?"

We all looked at the rabbi, who broke out into a big smile. His face began to shine so bright that you could almost measure it with a light meter as he said, "It is much sooner than you think. Perhaps you will want to join your pastor and these women in the study of the Holy Scriptures and learn more." Then he walked out. The older man stood up and said, "Come on, babe, let's see what the preacher has to say."

I quickly paid my bill and ran out after the rabbi because I had a lot of questions to ask him. But I was too late; he was nowhere to be found. I asked a local person standing nearby if he had seen a young man walk out of the café, and if he'd happened to notice the direction he was headed. He said that I was the only one who had walked out of the café in the last half hour. Such is my luck. But, boy, that young man had looked familiar. I just could not place where I had seen him before.

I got back into my car, and God was waiting for me to continue our journey. I said, "Lord, You should have been there." He replied, "I was."

32

OOH AND AAH

"Before I formed thee in the belly I knew thee;
and before thou camest forth out of the womb I sanctified thee."
—Jeremiah 1:5

This morning, as I sat in my cabin with my laptop, looking out the window at the Catskills, I felt God was trying to tell me something. Suddenly, I saw some leaves floating to the ground. I thought it was a little early for the leaves to be falling. As I watched those three or four leaves fall gracefully, almost poetically, to the ground, I began to think how it was only God and I who saw those particular leaves float down. No one else in the world saw those very leaves fall to the ground in their showcase of color.

As I experienced the unspeakable joy of the Lord in silence, I sensed His longing to share this experience. So I sit here just writing about it, hoping that maybe someone will read it (which turns out to be you!), hoping that they might have just a glimpse of the glory and beauty of the God whom we love and share.

This reminds me that, on my way to the Catskills, I made a brief side trip to take a tour of the home of author Washington Irving near Sleepy Hollow. At the end of the tour, the guide said we were welcome to stay and sit on a bench outside Irving's home overlooking the Hudson River. What writer would not jump at the opportunity to spend a few moments outside the home of one of America's classic authors and observe the scenes that had inspired his writings? Yet as I sat outside Washington Irving's home, looking out over the Hudson, resting in a place where he might have sat two hundred years ago, I came to realize that the pleasure of that moment was not as enjoyable by myself as it would have been if it had been shared with another person. If we are made in the image of God, perhaps He is not all that different from us in our desire to share something beautiful and glorious with someone else. Maybe, as I expressed earlier, that is one reason why God has brought me up here to the Catskills. He just wants to show off a little and have someone around to share in the beauty of His creation as it goes through the season of change from green to a glorious kaleidoscope of color. Maybe He just wants to sit with someone, someone whom He loves and will love Him in return, and together just watch a few leaves flutter to the ground.

More leaves are falling now. Sometimes the leaves fall gracefully, sometimes comically. Some fall when the winds blow, and they seem to chase after each other, racing to see which can make it to the ground first. Some just plop right down in front of you. Yet each one gives a little performance, like a model striding down the runway of a fashion show, providing a full display of its wonderful color.

Still more leaves are falling. They are coming down faster and in greater numbers, building up to a great crescendo, with God and I delighting in each one—laughing and oohing and aahing at their beauty. A few weeks ago, I observed a fireworks display created by human beings. Man can create a fireworks display that hundreds, even thousands, will crowd together to watch. Yet God is putting on this colorful display of leaves, which is even more beautiful, and it is only He and I who are watching.

Just as each leaf is different from any other—whether slightly or profoundly so—we, too, are slightly or profoundly different from the other billions of people whom God has created. At home, in the Chicago area, I drive a bus for the disabled each morning, and while I drive, I see young students going off to school. And there are millions just like them across the globe. To me, the students all look the same, but they are not; each one is distinct. Each one carries their own little backpack, and each has been dressed by a loving parent or guardian who purchased that little outfit from their hard-earned money, thinking how darling their child would look in it. Essentially, each is dressed for the pleasure of the one who loves them.

In Jeremiah 1:5, God told the prophet Jeremiah that He had "*formed*" him. The Hebrew term translated as "*formed*" is *yatsar*, which is a word used for a potter who fashions a vessel of clay. God's creation of us is not cookie-cutter, mass production; it is not the construction of little ticky-tacky, box houses on a hillside, each one identical to the next. Every one of the seven billion people on earth is individually made, handcrafted by the Master Potter, made at His desire and to His personal liking and purpose. In the original Hebrew text, the word *yatsar* occurs twice. This was done for emphasis, to make sure we noticed, and were particularly aware of, the fact that we are custom-built, specifically made for God's pleasure.

God molded us, designed us, custom-built us "*in the belly,*" as the King James Version renders it. The word for "*belly*" is *batan*, which is often translated *womb*; however, in its Semitic root, it refers to the seat of hunger or desire. The womb is the place where the longing desire of a man and woman who have shared intimacy hope to find the product of their intimacy, something tangible that they can love together. Likewise, God formed and customized us, making each of us special and unique out of a desire or longing to create something made in His image, something tangible, that He could love.

God also said to Jeremiah, "*Before thou camest forth out of the womb I sanctified thee.*" It is interesting that when we get to the word that is rendered "*womb*" in the King James Version, it turns out not really to be the word for womb at all; it is rarely used for that term. The word that the KJV translators, for whatever reason, rendered as "*womb*" is *racham*. It is one of the Hebrew words for love. This word is often translated as tender mercies; it is a romantic type of love; it is a tender, caring love. It is the love between a husband and wife, or between a mother and her baby.

Thus, even before God brought us forth out of a tender, caring love, He formed us to bring Him a special joy, a specific joy, that none of His other created beings could bring Him. Each of us, among the billions that He creates, is formed in a distinct way. Every person is a specially crafted individual whom He has made with a heart filled with love, to bring Him a joy that no one else in the world could bring Him.

What's more, it says that before bringing us forth, He *"sanctified"* us. The English word *sanctified* sounds so mysterious to us. We rarely use this word outside a church context, and it really has such an esoteric sound to it. The Hebrew word for *"sanctified"* is *qadash*, which means to be sacred, hallowed, or held up as something very special—so special that you treat it differently, carefully, and respectfully. Amazingly, that description refers to you and me. Each of us is sacred, hallowed, and held up as something special. Yes, little old bumbling, eccentric, foolish me, God considers as something very sacred to bring Him joy.

33

"YOU'RE A BETTER MAN, GUNGA DIN"

"Then said I, Ah, Lord God! behold,
I cannot speak: for I am a child."
—Jeremiah 1:6

One of the great lessons that the Catskills have been teaching me is just how small and insignificant I am in light of this great, majestic beauty of God's creation. I wonder if He could ever use someone as small and as imperfect as I am to accomplish anything for His kingdom.

Before I left for the Catskills, I watched an old movie called *Gunga Din* (pronounced "deen"), which was very loosely based on Rudyard Kipling's poem by the same name. The last lines of the poem, however, were quoted in the movie, and really expressed the true nature of the British soldier who lamented the death of the water bearer who had saved his life, while pondering the unsolved riddle of love. Unlike the Cary Grant character, who was very benevolent to Gunga Din, the soldier in the poem had been very cruel, abusive, and condescending to the young Indian servant whose only job was to carry water for the soldiers. Yet, this humble servant laid down his life to spare the life of that British soldier. The soldier had only seen an ignorant, uncouth, Indian servant who did not have the dignity of a British military officer. He had viewed him as someone whose only value in life was to do menial tasks for the soldiers. Yet in the end, this officer realized that Gunga Din was just as much a creation of God as he was, and that in the long run, this humble servant was a better man than he.

> Tho' I've belted you an' flayed you,
> By the livin' Gawd that made you,
> You're a better man than I am, Gunga Din![7]

As I reflected on Kipling's poem, I could not help but think again of Jeremiah. Jeremiah never really wanted to be a prophet. I was told in Bible college that he resisted the call because he knew of its dangers. Yet when I analyze Jeremiah 1:6, I see more of a picture of a man who was like Gunga Din. It wasn't so much that he was afraid as that he felt totally inadequate.

We are often led to believe that God dragged poor Jeremiah into the prophetic ministry kicking and screaming. Yet look again at his response to his call: *"Ah, Lord GOD! behold, I cannot speak: for I am a child."* The word translated *"child"* is *na'ar*, which could mean either a servant or a young maiden. It is not your typical word for a child, which is *yalad*. *Na'ar* comes from an old Persian word meaning to boil. In other Semitic languages, it has the idea of being agitated or stirred up, which is also a picture of boiling water. It eventually came to be associated with a young child or baby who is constantly stirred up, crying and whining. It is often used in the Hebrew and Aramaic for a baby of about three months old. Therefore, what Jeremiah is saying is that he could not be a prophet because he is as helpless as a three-month-old baby, who cannot even speak. The word rendered *"speak"* is *dabar*, whose spelling signifies words spoken from the heart. Jeremiah is basically saying that he cannot even express his own heart, so how is he going to express the heart of God?

We really get the true motive behind his response from the use of the word *"Ah."* The Hebrew word for this is *'ahah*, which is an interjection that expresses helplessness and self-pity. Jeremiah is really saying, "Oh, Lord, I am just a simple man. I cannot speak eloquently like those other prophets; I am not gifted and talented like they are. I mean, look at these others who call themselves prophets—when they prophesy, it is like pure poetry flowing from their lips. They are charismatic, handsome, and flamboyant, and I am just a simple Gunga Din with no other talent than to bear water for these other warriors." Yet God responds by saying, *"Be not afraid of their faces: for I am with thee to deliver thee"* (Jeremiah 1:8). The word for *"with*

---

7. Rudyard Kipling, "Gunga Din," 1890. See http://www.bartleby.com/103/48.html.

thee" is *'iteka*, which means more than just "with you"; it is an expression that means, "I am in a relationship with you; I am as near to you as your heart."

With that assurance, Jeremiah set forth on his prophetic ministry, only to be mocked, ridiculed, and tossed into prison. Yet, in the end, God did a mighty work from this humble man who felt he was so small and insignificant.

I look around at the mighty mountains and the moving streams, and I cry out, "Who am I that God could use me?" Yet God is saying that I am His instrument, and that whatever I accomplish in life will be done through Him, in His power and might. I have a relationship with Him, and He is near to me—as close to me as my own heart.

34

THERE IS A RIVER

"There is a river,
the streams whereof shall make glad the city of God."
—Psalm 46:4

"As the hart [deer] panteth after the water brooks,
so panteth my soul after thee, O God."
—Psalm 42:1

As I ponder my last day in the Catskills, I find there is still something very unsettled deep within my spirit. I hear myself crying out, "Oh, God, I don't want to leave You. I don't want to return to a life where I don't feel Your presence as I do now. Are You really going to leave me when I depart from the mountains?" Instantly, my thoughts went back to when I was a small child. Hanging on a wall in my bedroom was a small plaque placed there by my mother. It was actually very cheaply made; my mother used to lead the kindergarten class at vacation Bible school, and I think this was one of the craft projects they did where the children were given a wooden plaque to paint and put stickers on. The plaque in my room was probably the one my mother made as a demonstration. The sticker was of a little deer, and underneath she had written the words, "I will never leave you."

I looked out over the stream behind my cabin one last time, and I was reminded of Psalm 46:4: *"There is a river, the streams whereof shall make glad the city of God."* The word translated *"river"* in this verse is *nahar*, and as I described earlier, *nahar* can be rendered river or stream. It is a gentle, flowing, endless stream. I felt that God was saying to me, "Wherever you go, I will go with you, and My waters will never run dry."

The book of John tells about a woman from Samaria who met Jesus at a well. (See John 4:4–26.) This woman had been married five times, and the man she was currently living with was not her husband. Her situation was less an indication that she was an adulterous woman than it was a sign that she had been rejected. In those days, a woman could not live alone; she had to live in the household of the man responsible for taking care of her, such as a husband, father, or brother. Apparently, after this woman's first husband had died or left her, she had been bounced around from husband to husband, no more than a servant or a slave to them. When one man grew tired of her, she was passed along to another. Yet Jesus broke the social protocols of the day—men not talking to women publicly, and Jews not interacting with Samaritans—and took the time to speak to her. For a Jewish man to speak to a Samaritan woman in that culture was definitely not politically correct.

Jesus told the woman that He would give her *"living water"* (John 4:10), a gift from God, and that if she were to drink this water, she would never thirst again (see verse 14). I know what Jesus was talking about, because when I first came to the Catskill Mountains, I was spiritually thirsty, and that thirst was not quenched until I drank from the living waters of Jesus Christ. Yet, if that thirst is quenched, why do I have this unsettling feeling in my spirit? I believe it is a call to closet myself in Jesus, to know Him in a much deeper, more intimate way.

Still, there has been a quenching of my thirst here in the Catskills, and that quenching reminds me of something Horatio Spafford expressed. Spafford was a well-known lawyer from Chicago in the nineteenth century whose wife and four daughters were in a shipwreck; of his whole family, his wife alone survived. He boarded another ship in order to be with his wife, and when he passed over the spot in the ocean where his daughters had perished, he was able to say, because of his relationship with Jesus, "It is well with my soul." Thus, I know I can leave this retreat of peace and comfort to return to whatever I must face in the next year, knowing that "it is well with my soul." Yet I am still driven to bathe in the living waters of God.

After I left my cabin and began driving home, I went by the stream that has kept me company this past week. And there by the stream was a deer. Of course, I immediately thought of Psalm 42:1: *"As the hart [deer] panteth after the water brooks, so panteth my soul after thee, O God."* The word translated *"panteth"* in this verse is *'arak*. It comes from an ancient Persian word meaning to arise. In Hebrew, it has the idea of an arousal, a rising of passion or desire. That little deer had come out of hiding because he was *panting* of thirst. His sole passion at that moment was to get a drink of water. Similarly, my soul is panting for more of God. I have come out of my hiding in the Catskills only to find more of His living waters to drink.

I pulled over and parked near the stream in order to watch the deer, and he looked up at me. I felt in my heart that he was saying, "Watch me as I drink this water." Then he lowered his head to the stream and began to lap up water. Not quickly, not desperately, but slowly, enjoying every little drop. I felt my little friend was telling me that my thirst for God was not just a side trip on my journey through life—a quick gulp to quench my thirst before I moved on. Drinking of the living waters was meant to be fully enjoyed as my thirst was continually quenched.

Yes, God intends to fill us with His living water, but not just so that we can be filled, like filling our car at a gas station to help us continue our journey. This is meant to be an *'arak*. Each sip is not meant to just satisfy us, but also to arouse in us a passion—a passion to savor every moment, every drop, of the living water, to keep drinking and keep coming back to the stream for more and more.

Accordingly, this living water is not to be tasted only on Sunday mornings during the worship time at church. You do not attend your Sunday worship to quench your thirst. That Sunday worship is the first sip of living water for the week. It not only satisfies, but it also builds in you a passion, a desire, for more and more. That worship service is an *'arak*; it arouses our passion and desire to go into the rest of the week seeking God in every corner and crevice of our daily life.

The deer finished taking his refreshment and then just looked at me. I looked back at him, and I suddenly realized that he was just like that little deer depicted in the picture that hung on my wall when I was a child. I began to listen with my heart, and it was as if I heard him speak words from the first Scripture verse I ever memorized: "Our Creator said He will never leave you nor forsake you." (See Hebrews 13:5.) Then he swiftly ran past me, with all the beauty and grace that God has bestowed upon him. I knew that even though I was leaving the Catskill Mountains, God would be going with me, that He would never leave me nor forsake me.

I leave for home now, not only having satisfied my longing for God's living waters, but also having received an 'arak, an elevation of my passion and desire for more, for experiencing the living, loving life of Jesus Christ in every situation I encounter in the remaining journey of my life through this world.

PART THREE
NEW SPIRITUAL DEPTHS

PROLOGUE: A RENEWED RELATIONSHIP WITH GOD

"Behold, the former things are come to pass, and new things do I declare: before they spring forth I tell you of them."
—Isaiah 42:9

I am about to leave for my second visit to the Abbey of Gethsemani in a little more than two years to spend another week there in silence. I am facing new beginnings—new things are entering my life so quickly that I must take a break and go on this silent retreat so I can be sure I am really hearing God's voice.

Judging from the mail I receive, it appears I am not the only one looking forward to some new things. People of all ages have written to me, talking about their need for a new beginning or for something new to come into their lives. Well, Isaiah 42:9 is the verse to claim. Not only does it promise new things, but it also says that God will tell us about them before they happen.

Okay, here it comes: *we need to look at the context of the verse.* Don't you just hate that? A perfectly good promise to claim, and we have to look at the context. But, hey, if this was meant only for Isaiah's time, then why is it in the Bible? There must be a present-day application.

The context indicates that it is the prophet Isaiah who is speaking the words of the Lord, and God is saying that now that His prophecies of the past have come to fruition, what He is about to say will also come to pass. Through Isaiah, God is expressing something here that is perhaps a little odd—that He will declare the *"new things,"* and before they actually happen, He will tell us about them. That may sound somewhat contradictory. If He is going to declare the new things, isn't that the same as telling us about the new things? To better understand what God is saying here, let's explore the deeper meanings of some of the words in this statement.

The Hebrew word translated *"declare"* is *negad*, which means to tell or speak out in clear, straightforward terms. The word is in a hiphal participle form, so God is presently declaring new things, and He is making it very clear what these new things will be. The word translated *"new things"* is *chadesh*, whose root word means to restore or to renew. The Hebrew letters of this word would suggest that these new things are in regard to one's relationship with God. The first letter is chet, which represents a bonding with God; and we will accomplish that bonding by passing through what the second letter, the daleth, signifies, which is a doorway to what the third letter, shin, symbolizes, which is peace and fulfillment found only in Him. Additionally, *chadesh* is in a hiphal form, which suggests an excitement or anticipation on the part of God. In other words, He is so excited about our forthcoming new relationship with Him that He is declaring it before it even happens.

The Hebrew word translated *"spring forth"* is *tsamek*, which has the idea of sprouting. Prior to these new things beginning to sprout, God will announce them. The word for *"tell"* is *shama'*, which carries more of the idea of hearing than speaking; it, too, is in a hiphal form. Thus, God will do something that will cause us to "hear," or to be aware, of these new things.

Again, the hiphal forms of *negad* and *shama'* would seem to suggest God's excitement and expectation about this new relationship. What is God communicating in this passage? A picture is being drawn here of a bridegroom anticipating the fulfillment of his relationship with his bride. As the bridegroom proposes or accepts the arrangement of marriage with his beloved, he declares, "I am taking for myself a bride." He makes this fact clear and plain to all. Everyone rejoices, and preparations for the wedding begin.

Much of the rest of Isaiah 42 goes into detail about these *"new things"* that God is going to do, or the wedding plans and events that will unfold before the wedding actually takes place. However, it can all be summarized in the idea of God restoring, *chadesh*, His relationship with mankind. The thing that stands out to me is that this is not a picture of God pushing buttons and pulling levers in order to bring everything to a conclusion. It is more a picture of a wonderful play that God is directing, with a beautiful storyline about the preparation for a wedding. There are a lot of villains and twists and turns in the plot. Yet, the whole time, there is a growing anticipation on God's part for the last scene, when the groom finally comes for his bride and their marriage is consummated.

Thus, God is depicted here as a wonderful storyteller who is anxiously awaiting the final act and scene when He can establish Himself as the true hero of the story. We tend to forget that He is a Bridegroom. (See, for example, Revelation 19:9.) The bridegroom looks forward to his wedding day just as much as the bride does. And God is just as anxious as we are to bring all this to a conclusion, for us to reach that final consummation with Him. Even before it springs forth, or begins to bud, He is anticipating and listening, as a bridegroom anticipates and listens for his bride. He is enjoying that period before the wedding when He sees and hears His bride happily preparing for that day, and He rejoices in knowing that He is the reason for her happiness and anticipation.

Let me make a personal application here. Sure, I want certain changes in my life; there are many things I want to be different. But if I do experience changes or a new level in my relationship with God, I have a feeling that all the changes I desire will take place as a result of that relationship, just as a woman's relationship with her fiancé is transformed when he takes her as his bride. Her life often changes completely—she has a new home, a new family, and a new life all at once. Old things pass away, and everything becomes new. (See 2 Corinthians 5:17.) The bridegroom is not slack in hinting of this coming change. The look in his eye, the tone of his voice, and his slightest touch are filled with passion, and they arouse passion in his beloved. Thus, as I am about to go through some simple changes—moving into a new apartment, having a new book released, developing new fellowships—in each case, I sense God getting excited over what is about to take place. I really have no idea what is next, but all this is happening at the same time I am going off to spend a week in silence with Him, and Him alone.

For all of us, our time on earth is merely a period of preparation for our wedding with Jesus, our Bridegroom. As with the preparations for any wedding, there can be difficulties and trials involved. Additionally, as the day of a wedding grows closer, there are many exchanges between the bride and groom as they experience the growing realization that their relationship will soon be consummated. Right now is that time for us and God, because He is anticipating these *"new things"* just as much as we are.

I must be honest: since my last visit to the abbey, I have lost much of the glow that I shared with God at that time. I am looking forward to a *chadesh*—a renewed relationship with God. Therefore, I go to the abbey fully expecting to hear God declare the change that will take place in my relationship with Him, and I know that this change will correspond to a change in my life. But, you know what? I am so excited over the coming transformation in my relationship with God that I don't care about the other changes that will take place in my life, for better or for worse.

35

TRAIN UP

*"Train up a child in the way he should go: and when he is old, he will
not depart from it."*
—Proverbs 22:6

I f you are in any way remotely involved in the children's ministries of your
church, you will most likely hear someone quote the above verse as your
incentive to teach the children placed under your care. I have no doubt
that this verse is applicable to any situation where you are charged with
instructing or caring for children. However, we probably didn't need Solomon to tell us this, because we already know it based on our own experiences. For example, many of us who attended Sunday school or some club
program at church while we were growing up were aware of the fact that
what the teachers and leaders said or did could affect a child for the rest
of his life. This leads me to believe there is a little more to this verse than
meets the eye.

The Hebrew word translated *"child"* is *na'ar*, which can signify either a
male or female child or an infant. The word for *"train up"* is *chanak*, which,
in its Semitic root, has the idea of a "narrowing." Children have a wide
range of choices to make, and it is their parents, teachers, and other leaders
who help them to narrow the choices to *"the way* [they] *should go."*

Chanak, or *"train up,"* also contains the idea of experiencing something.
Much of the training that adults give children comes in the form of giving
them the opportunity to experience the way they should go. Experience is
the best teacher. For instance, a science teacher can explain the result of a

science experiment, but when the students themselves can perform that experiment, they will experience the result firsthand and will likely never forget it. I recall attending Beginners' Sunday School at my church when I was growing up, and coloring pictures of Moses and the fiery bush or the golden calf. All those times of coloring still linger in my mind and help me to recall the biblical stories.

Chanak has one other meaning: the idea of being tried. A wise parent or instructor will allow a child to fail and will encourage the child to try again. The process of trying and trying again is another great teacher.

Thus, in Proverbs 22:6, the statement about training children includes the ideas of helping them to narrow their choices so they can choose the correct way, giving them the opportunity to experience their choice, allowing them to fail, and encouraging them to try and try again. Perhaps you can testify to the profound effect such a pattern of training had on you at an early age and how it shaped your life.

Now let's look at the last part of the verse: "*When he is old, he will not depart from it.*" According to the Hebrew, another way of translating the phrase "*when he is old*" is, "even when he is old," and some Bible versions render it that way. To merely say "when he is old" is to suggest that the child will fall away but will eventually return. Although that certainly does happen with some people, I know that in my case, I never fell away from my early training, and I know many others who have stayed true to the faith they were raised in. So, for us, "even when he is old" applies. However, the beauty of the Hebrew language is that you can equally translate the phrase "*when he is old.*" Accordingly, even if a child falls away, he will return.

What does all this have to do with my entering a new period of silence before God and anticipating a renewed relationship with Him? It seems the first thing on God's agenda was to take me back to the day when faith was simple and easy for me—to the time before I took my first theology class, or my first Hebrew and Greek courses, to the period before my faith took on such a complexity. God wanted me to remember a day before I pondered what "predestination" or "the perseverance of the saints" meant, before I began to wonder whether epistemology was really a presupposition for neoorthodoxy. He desired to take me back to a time when I sang

"The B-I-B-L-E" in Tiny Tots and held up my Bible, learning to love that Book so much that I devoted my life to studying it. To a time when I heard the story of Jonah in the belly of a whale—with my teacher illustrating the account with flannelgraphs—and didn't wonder how a guy could last three days in a fish's stomach without the acids dissolving him. To a time when my class sang "Jesus Loves the Little Children of the World," and we thought about Jesus's love, not about whether or not the song might be racist; when we sang "Climb, Climb Up Sunshine Mountain" and didn't wonder what in the world Sunshine Mountain was. To a day when, in primary Sunday school, I cut out pictures of Jesus and pasted them in a little scrapbook. When I memorized Bible verses to get merit badges for Awana Club, having little idea at the time what the verses meant, but fifty years later having those verses come back to my mind when I needed them the most. When a man named Wayne Kemp played the piano for the youth, and we gathered around, singing choruses late into the night. When our intermediate Sunday school superintendent, Herman Bell, would take us to Chinatown if we memorized our Bible verses and had perfect Sunday school attendance. When our junior church superintendent, Bill Pointer, taught us to sing "Nothing Is Impossible." When leaders Chuck and Robbie and my parents took the young people on weekly social activities and yearly retreats. When little white-gloved ladies assured me that God had a great plan for my life and that they were praying for me, and when I could generate a big smile and a "Praise the Lord" from them when I said I was planning to go to Moody Bible Institute and become a pastor, and even draw a tear or two when I added that I might do some missionary work.

On my trip here to the abbey, I drove through the countryside of various Southern states, and I listened to a radio station that played all the old gospel music and hymns that I had grown up with, transporting me back to the day when I had that simple faith, a faith that never questioned, a faith that humbly believed in God and loved Him with all my heart. Yet I was also taken back to the time not too long ago when my world collapsed, my marriage fell apart, my career was in shambles, my finances were a mess, and my future looked hopeless. It was a time when I began to question the reality of my faith and wondered if God even existed. A time when I cried out to Him, "Just where is my faith?" That is when God took me back to the times I just described—the days of singing those gospel choruses, pasting those little pictures of Jesus into a scrapbook, singing around the piano, trips to Chinatown, Friday night youth activities, and weekend retreats. Jesus spoke to my heart and said, "There is your faith; it was implanted in your heart because you attended a church where people loved you, prayed for you, and *trained* you, *chanak*, in the way you should go. No sweat; you're okay. Your faith is intact."

So I go into my time of silence before God with just a simple, childlike faith. I am ready to believe, like a child, that God can use His birds and animals to speak to me about His wonders; ready to believe that a tree or a field of green grass can cry out to me of God's love and care; ready to believe that God speaks to me in little coincidences and in everything that quickens my spirit; ready to believe that Jesus will be in the meditation room every morning waiting for me to sit down and just talk with Him; ready to believe that "Jesus loves me, this I know, for the Bible tells me so."[8]

---

8. Anna B. Warner, "Jesus Loves Me," 1860.

36

NO DIVERSIONS

"Then the king went to his palace and spent the night fasting; no diversions were brought to him, and sleep fled from him."
—Daniel 6:18 (ESV)

The first thing I noticed when I arrived at the abbey was that both my iPhone and iPad showed a little notification saying, "No Service." Once again, I was truly shut off from society. When I spent time in silence in the Catskills, I still had Internet access and therefore had a link to the outside world. Here, I had nothing like that. I had entered a place with no radios, no television, virtually no Internet service (I did discover one room with Internet access), or anything else that might distract someone. And the last words I spoke for this entire week were to Father Braddock, who gave me the key to my room and blessed me. Before God, I have taken a vow of silence for the duration of my stay. No words will pass my lips, no music will come from my iPad; I will live in absolute silence before the Lord. There will be no distractions.

In this context, it is curious that I am reading Daniel 6:18, which describes the king of Persia—who had been forced to sentence Daniel to the lions' den—going to his chambers and fasting. The verse says that *"no diversions were brought to him."* Some Bible translations say there were no musical instruments played. The king sought nothing that would distract him from his troubled mind. Daniel 6 is among those chapters in the book of Daniel that were originally written in Aramaic. The Aramaic word translated as *"diversions"* is *'alal*, which means to work, to do deeds, to create a distraction, or to be entertained. Essentially, the king of Persia went into his chambers and told his administrative assistant that he was taking no calls.

If the king was as troubled and anxious as Scripture indicates he was, then he could have made himself extremely busy in order to get his mind off of Daniel's predicament. But he didn't. Yet merely sitting alone in his room fretting about it would do no good, and I just can't believe that the mightiest king on the planet, a leader of men, would use his time fretting. There were many things going on that demanded his attention, and, as king, he would not have wasted this time. Thus, he must have been doing something more than just sitting on his bed worrying. I know I am just guessing, but I suspect he knew about the Jewish practice of silence and therefore spent the night in silence before God Jehovah with his petition for Daniel's safety. The Bible does not specifically say this, but I certainly assume it, although I may be reading into it. He was cutting himself off from all distractions so he could focus his whole attention on God and present his request before Him.

As for me, I am having some difficulty readjusting to living with "no diversions." I have been at the abbey now for three hours, and I am bored to death! An hour ago, I ran out of things to pray about; I am prayed out. There is nothing to do here except walk around the compound looking forward to lunch. However, because I've been in silence before, I know it takes a little time to become used to this way of life and get your mind stayed on the Lord. I know I have to become focused on my relationship with God. I need to find a way to reestablish a close connection with Him. It is sort of like a first date—you are fishing around for a subject that you are both interested in, but once you find it, the conversation takes care of itself.

During my drive to the abbey, in addition to listening to gospel music and hymns, I listened to a radio preacher talk about marriage. He said that in all his years of marriage counseling and observing marriages, he found that the most successful relationships always had their routines, certain things the couple enjoyed doing together regularly. It might be a morning greeting with a kiss or a hug. It might be reading the Bible or praying together. It might be walking the dog or just sitting out on the porch, holding hands. It might be having dinner together, sometimes with both husband and wife cooking the meal together before they sit down to enjoy the food and each other's company. Thus, every successful marriage has its routines, things the couple frequently does together, things they both enjoy doing. These little rituals, these routine acts, are anticipated by both husband and wife, and it causes them to watch the clock for the times when they can share them.

You know, there's nothing wrong with ritual in religion, either, as long as you practice it as a special event in which you celebrate your love for God. I drive a woman on my disability bus to Mass a couple of times a week. There is a sign at her church that says, "Saturday evening Mass — fulfills Sunday obligation." I asked her why she goes during the week since she is only obligated to attend once a week. She replied, "Oh, I don't go under any obligation. I go because it is a time God and I get together; it is our little routine." Say what you will about Mass, I believe God takes great delight in celebrating the Mass with this little lady. The ceremony is just the act; what is important is the bonding taking place between God and this woman. It is a little ritual performed out of love.

When such established rituals are neglected—rituals with either a loved one or with God—then something in the relationship can be lost. Suppose a husband writes his wife a little poem or story every day as one of their shared rituals. If, on a particular day, the husband did not have a poem or story ready (without a good reason), his wife would be disappointed; it would be a kind of violation of their mutual love and understanding. It's not that she *needs* a little poem or story, but rather that her lover missed something that was a custom between them and that she had come to anticipate as a demonstration of his love.

Thinking about these things, I asked God if there was any routine He would enjoy having us do together this week. He led me to a tree I remembered from my first visit—the white tree. I had never really explored this tree on my first visit, so I decided to look at it more closely this time around. It was not a white birch or another tree whose bark is white by nature. It had practically no bark on it. I noticed that the white color appeared to be almost painted on. I know the brothers here practice various sciences, such as astronomy and botany. I assume one of the brothers is an amateur botanist and took a special liking to this tree. It might have been dying and losing its bark, and because bark is a special protection for a tree, he substituted some other kind of protection for it.

Regardless, I sensed the Lord was saying, "This is our routine: come to this tree every morning, and we shall talk. I have many things to talk about and to teach you from this great white tree."

37

THE LEAST

"And the King shall answer and say unto them, Verily I say unto you,
Inasmuch as ye have done it unto one of the least of these my brethren,
ye have done it unto me."
—Matthew 25:40

I was sitting in front of the great white tree, my new special meeting place with God, and I was thrilling over this experience of being alone with Him, just He and I together. I reflected on how nice it would be to live the rest of my life this way, on the mountaintop, and not have to go back to the valley and face the problems and heartaches of this world.

Suddenly, a little bird flew down near me and began to chirp and move around as if it were dancing. The Talmud teaches that when a bird lands near you and acts in this way, it is trying to get your attention to tell you that the Holy Spirit is near. Well, the Holy Spirit dwells inside me, so I figured God was trying to get my attention. I said, "Okay, Lord, it is Your turn. Tell me what You want me to know and understand."

The Lord reminded me of something I had observed at a rest area off the interstate on my drive down to the abbey. I had seen a young father and his little son, who was about two years old, rolling a ball back and forth to each other. The little child was laughing with delight, and the father was enjoying every moment. Sitting on top of a picnic table nearby was the mother, watching this interaction between father and son. Her face was glowing with joy and pleasure over watching her husband and little child play together. My spirit was quickened, and I heard the Lord say to me, "You see how happy this young wife and mother is, yet neither her child nor her husband is paying any attention to her or including her in the activity. She is left out of the game, yet she is filled with joy over watching the father of her child play with him. She has her own time alone with her husband, and they share some very tender moments together. But if her husband were to give all his attention to her and neglect their child, she would be greatly disappointed, and the attention her husband gave her would be unwelcome. So, too, with Me. I have many children I want to reach, and I want you to reach out to them to enjoy their fellowship, for it gives Me great pleasure watching you interact with My children."

I asked the Lord what the great white tree had to do with this. Then I thought about how, the weekend before, I had visited the Appalachian Mountains, and a new friend had taken me to a place where we were able to look out over a forest of trees. I had commented that the pine trees looked like they were dying, because all the branches seemed to be dead except the ones toward the tops of the trees. She told me this was because sunlight was not able to reach the lower portions, but that the trees were actually quite healthy, and that you can always tell the health of a tree by the growth at its top.

I looked once more at the great white tree. It had many dead branches on it, but toward the top, there were green leaves. The Lord spoke to me again and said, "You are in the Sonlight right now, and you are flourishing, but look at the branches below you; they have no leaves because they have no Sonlight. I need you to bring my Sonlight to them so that they, too, will know the joy that I have for them. I do enjoy our time together, but you must return to the valley, bringing to them the Sonlight that you have found here."

I thought of Matthew 25:40, where Jesus said, "*Inasmuch as ye have done it unto one of the least of these my brethren, ye have done it unto me.*" In Greek, the language of the New Testament, the word for "*least*" here is *elachistos*, which means to be inferior. However, in Aramaic, the language that Jesus spoke, the word for "*least*" is *zeora*, which means little, least, or few, but in the sense of having little knowledge or ability to work through difficulties or gain understanding. When you help someone who is helpless, that person is usually grateful and joyful. Thus, the verse could actually read, "As you have brought joy to another, you have brought joy to Me."

The word for "*brethren*" in Matthew 25:40 is *adelphos*, which means just that—brethren. Regarding the term for "brother" in Aramaic, it is curious that the word is *akaya*, which is generally used in relation to someone with whom you have gone through a difficult crisis. For example, soldiers will sometimes call themselves *brothers-in-arms*. They have shared in conflict and war, and their suffering and comradeship have created a bond between them almost like that of kinsmen. Therefore, I believe Jesus was referring here to our giving aid and helpful knowledge to those who have bonded with Him in the fellowship of His sufferings. (See Philippians 3:10.) Jesus knows and understands heartbreak, rejection, and physical suffering, and He has a bond with those who have experienced similar things. They are His *akaya*, and when we reach out to those who have suffered as Jesus did, we are bringing comfort to Him as well.

So ends my first lesson at the great white tree. During my time of silence, I am receiving the full force of Sonlight, experiencing the joy and pleasure of the Lord in this atmosphere where there are no distractions. However, the retreat will end in a few days, and I must return to share that Sonlight with Jesus's *zeora*, the "least" who are out of reach of the Sonlight; with Jesus's *akaya*, His brothers in suffering. For if I can bring some relief to their difficulties and suffering, I have brought relief and joy to Him in His own suffering over their tragic or distressing circumstances.

38

JESUS WEPT

"Jesus wept."
—John 11:35

It is a cold, dark, and rainy day, and I am sitting on the porch looking out at the gloom. I don't believe that God brought this gloomy weather just for me, but I do believe He uses circumstances to teach and direct us. Since He knew it would be this type of day today, He led me to be here at the abbey in order to reveal the reason why He called me back into silence.

Someone once said that it always rains on Good Friday because the rain is like God crying. Well, a glance at the meteorological records for the past hundred years, or for however long they have been keeping such records, would show that there has never been a Good Friday when it has rained all over the world. Still, it is a nice thought—even though the death of Jesus is not ultimately to be considered a sad event to weep over, but rather a joyful one, for it was His death and resurrection that gave the world freedom from spiritual death.

Nonetheless, the idea of God weeping echoes a truth that the Lord revealed to me in my previous visit to the abbey, one that He is expanding upon now. In John 11:35, we read that *"Jesus wept."* The Greek word translated *"wept"* in this verse is *edakrusen*. Two verses earlier, in John 11:33, which records Mary telling Jesus that her brother, Lazarus, had died, it says Mary was *"weeping"*; but, in that instance, the Greek word is *klaiontas*. Some translations render this word as a "lamenting" in order to indicate that two different words were used to translate "weep." It is that way in the

Aramaic, too. But although both Greek words literally mean crying, the two words do not indicate different degrees in the intensity of the tears, but rather the different focus of the tears.

When Jesus *edakrusen*, or wept, He was not weeping because He Himself was grief-stricken or because His own heart was broken. He was weeping over the broken hearts of Mary and those who wept with her over the loss of their relative and friend. Jesus knew Lazarus was in a good place, but the sadness of Mary and the other Jews broke His heart. When Mary and the Jews *klaiontas*, they were weeping for themselves and their own broken hearts.

Sitting here on the porch on this rainy day, I see birds of various varieties flying back and forth, landing at the feeders, eating, and then flying away. There are robins, sparrows, a cardinal, and even a mourning dove. Surely a mourning dove should pause and give a mournful coo over this dark and gloomy day; but alas, he, like the rest of the birds, seems totally oblivious to the rain. All the birds are just going about their business.

My spirit is quickened as I observe this. I recognize that I am like those birds. Jesus's heart is broken over a lost and dying world, yet I normally just go about my business, not thinking about Jesus's heart, but rather taking care to make sure I am well fed, secure, and comfortable in my life. By the way, my physical comforts have been challenged at the abbey. I was given permission to stay in the monks' section of the dormitory and not the more modern and updated dormitory provided for the retreatants. I had wanted to experience life like the monks. Big mistake. The heat has already been turned off in the archaic wing of the monastery, and it is unseasonably cold. I froze last night. I guess I am a spoiled American, used to the luxury of our modern technology, which keeps everything at a comfortable seventy-two degrees. Let it drop to around sixty degrees, and I am "suffering." On top of that, I was late for dinner yesterday, and by the time I arrived, there was really nothing left but some bread and peanut butter. So I went to bed cold *and* hungry, but the Lord reminded me that I was more comfortable than most of the people in the world whom He loves.

Thus, I am usually so focused on my own comfort in life that I spend much of the time crying *klaiontas* out of my own need but rarely crying *edakrusen* for the needs of others. I repented before God, saying, "Oh, precious Father, forgive me. I have been so self-focused and self-absorbed trying to make my few remaining years on this planet comfortable for myself that I am becoming much less aware of the tears that You cry for this lost world. Dear Father, let me enter Your heart; allow me to feel what Your heart feels—not just the joy, but the sorrow as well. Let me weep with You; let me weep with those who weep."

I suddenly find that the joy and peace I have been experiencing since my arrival at the abbey has gone. I am feeling restless, anxious, fearful. I find I have left the room in God's heart where there is dancing and celebration, and have entered a quiet room, His weeping room. That room is a reflection of the rainy, dark, gloomy day outside. The rain has become God's tears to me, and the birds have become the hearts of those for whom Jesus was weeping. One little robin has now approached me on the porch. He is looking at me with a mournful gaze, and he is shaking as if shivering from the cold. He pokes around the ground, trying to find some food. He finds a worm, but it escapes from him. Now he is hopping around, seeming almost desperate for nourishment, and I shed tears as I think of the multitudes who are so hungry for God but who are living with broken hearts, of those who are weeping because they have no job to support their families, of those throughout the world who have no food to eat. The little robin looks at me as if to ask, "Are you not going to offer me some bread?" Then he flies away. I could have saved some of the bread I had last evening, but I did not think to do that. I was too focused on myself. I was unprepared.

Similarly, we Christians are often unprepared to feed a lost and dying world because we are just so focused on ourselves. We are too busy singing and dancing to enter God's quiet room, His weeping room, in order to weep with Him for the lost.

39

ASK

"Ask, and it shall be given you; seek, and ye shall find;
knock, and it shall be opened unto you."
—Matthew 7:7

I am now in the weeping room of the heart of Jesus. He is sharing with me hearts that I have never met. He shows me the heart of a woman who was recently widowed. She is grief-stricken, worried, and fearful for her children. Her children are off at school, and she is sitting at home alone, shedding tears of sorrow, loneliness, hopelessness, and fear.

She is anxious. This morning, I woke up feeling the same anxiety, but I had nothing to be anxious about. I had a day free from worries, with no pressures and no stress here at the abbey. I should have been at peace. I recognized that I had entered God's weeping room, and I was feeling the anxiety experienced by this woman who had been left alone in the world. I felt the same abandonment, fear, and loneliness that she was feeling.

"Lord," I cried, "I came here expecting to have a joyful time. I expected this time to be filled with celebration and perhaps revelation, and now I find I have entered a world of sadness and heartbreak. Am I to spend the whole week feeling this sorrow and anxiety that is not my own?" Jesus answered, "I left My throne in heaven to come to this earth to feel what I could not feel in heaven. I wanted to feel your pain and your suffering. Is it too much to ask for you to do the same for others?"

"But," I argue, "what good does it do to feel another's suffering? I don't even know this woman. I've never met her, and I most likely never will.

What am I accomplishing by feeling her pain?" Jesus held her heart out to me and said, "Here, hold her heart in your hands as I continue to hold it." When I did, the grief, the heartbreak, and the fear I experienced were so intense that I cried out to Jesus, "Oh, my God, come help this wounded little lamb; come bring her peace, rest, and comfort." Then Jesus said, "I shall."

I knew without a doubt that a young widow somewhere in this world who had been crying her heart out had suddenly felt herself surrounded by the peace of God, that she was now rejoicing and praising God, and that Jesus was feeling her pleasure and joy. Instantly, I, too, was rejoicing, feeling that pleasure and joy. I have no idea where this woman lives, and I have no idea who she is, but I know she exists, and I know that I prayed for her and she was comforted.

Jesus then said, "You have not because you ask not.[9] This child of Mine was so filled with grief that she did not even think to call upon Me, and I could not help her unless she asked, because I have given everyone a free will. Yet you were in distress over this woman's suffering, and you asked for relief. The only way I could answer your request was to bring her comfort and peace. That is why you must learn to bear one another's burdens[10]—so you can pray such fervent prayers for others in need. Far too many people spend all their time saying words of praise to Me, which I appreciate, but they neglect to intercede, to stand in the gap, for those whom I long to comfort and save. It is a higher praise to Me when you share My burdens for those whom I love. That is the highest praise—when you share in My sufferings."

I have been reading Matthew 7:7: "*Ask, and it shall be given you; seek, and ye shall find; knock, and it shall be opened unto you.*" The word for "*ask*" in Aramaic is *sha'al*, which does not mean merely asking for something, but asking out of a real need. Of course, the very act of asking represents a certain need, but often that need is just to satisfy our curiosity or to receive some assistance to make life a little easier for us; the need is not really pressing. This word *sha'al* is asking for something more important and specific.

---

9. See James 4:2.
10. See Galatians 6:2.

The spelling of *sha'al* has a built-in commentary. It tells us what type of asking we are to do. The first letter is shin, which signifies the passionate love of God. The second letter, aleph, represents a unity with God, and the third letter, lamed, represents expressing one's heart to God. Thus, *sha'al* denotes to ask, but used in this context, it means asking for the passionate love of God; it means asking to be so unified with Him that you can express your heart to Him or His heart to you. In other words, if you ask from your heart, He will give what you request.

Too often, we do not make requests of God from our hearts, but rather from our minds. When I worked for Lester Sumrall Evangelistic Association (LeSEA), I would stand in the prayer line in their megachurch, and I would pray for people's needs. One time, a young man came forward and asked for prayer for healing from cancer. He didn't specify what type of cancer he had or where it was located, and I didn't ask. I merely started to pray out of duty. Suddenly, I thought, *I am wasting my time; I don't care about this man and his cancer, and I don't even know him. I am not praying from my heart, only from my mind.* I quickly asked the Lord to allow me to pray from my heart. Instantly, I felt a pain in my right side that was so great I could hardly breathe. When I finally got control of myself, I asked this man where the cancer was, and he said it was in his right side, in the very spot where I was feeling the pain. I was able to pray not only a sincere prayer, but a prayer that truly came from my heart, because I felt what that man felt. It was not pleasant, but you know what? I believe God found pleasure in that prayer, and I would gladly experience that pain again if it would bring about a prayer from my heart and a smile of pleasure from my God.

I made a promise to God that if He would allow me to enter His weeping room and share in His suffering and the suffering of others, I would *sha'al*, or offer a prayer from my heart. If He so desires, He can take all the joy I feel in my heart and give it to another person's heart, for finding that sorrowful heart filled with joy would only replenish the supply of joy I had just given away.

40

THE WEEPING TREE

"And it repented the LORD that he had made man on the earth,
and it grieved him at his heart."
—Genesis 6:6

In the above verse, the Hebrew word translated *"repented," nacham,* is not the word usually used to convey repentance. *Nacham* carries more of the idea of sorrow and grief than of turning away from something or of changing—although grieving over something you have done can often cause you to make a change or turn away from a certain thing. But again, that is not the emphasis of the word *nacham.*

Therefore, when we read that *"it repented the LORD that he had made man,"* it wasn't that God felt He had made a big mistake in creating humanity and had started to regret it. I believe God went into the creation of humanity with His eyes wide open. If not, He probably would have chucked the whole idea of human beings and their free will. Yet He chose not to because of one righteous man, Noah, who brought Him pleasure. (See Genesis 6:5–9.)

The fall of humanity and the resulting increased evil on the earth were tragic. Yet, in a sense, we cannot really know pleasure if we do not know sorrow. Thus, the sinfulness of man and the *nacham,* or grief, it created in God only seemed to have increased the pleasure He received from Noah's righteousness.

What I want to emphasize about this passage in Genesis is that God is an emotional God. He is a God who feels grief. We often tend to think of Him as a huge, unemotional giant who is just waiting for us to make one little slip up so He can send down His lightning bolts on us. Yet, even at the beginning of the history of mankind, we find that God was moved to grief over our sin. The Hebrew term translated *"grieved"* is *'atsab,* which is a word for intense emotional pain. In my writings, I have often described God as weeping. I do not believe God cries real tears, but He does experience many of the same emotions that create tears; when I say God "weeps," it is a humanization of those emotions. I picture God weeping because it helps me to understand His sorrow over us.

When I met with God today, I asked Him what it was that He particularly wanted me to learn this day from the white tree. I had no sooner asked the Lord that question when my attention was drawn to a weeping willow tree. One of the main Hebrew words used for "tree" in the Scriptures actually comes from the same Semitic root (no pun intended) as the word in Genesis 6:6 for *"grieved."* In the ancient world (as is frequently the case today), a tree was often a place of shade where one could go and sit and be alone to contemplate. Often, that contemplation involved sorrow; hence the reason "grieve" has the same root as "tree," which is *'ats.* The weeping willow tree, however, got its name because its branches are hanging down as if it is weeping. Still, my spirit was quickened at the sight of the weeping willow tree next to the white tree that has lost its bark.

In my book *Hebrew Word Study: Revealing the Heart of God,* I have a chapter on Song of Solomon 4:9, which says, *"Thou hast ravished my heart, my sister, my spouse; thou hast ravished my heart with one of thine eyes, with one chain of thy neck."* With just one glance, one look of love at Solomon, a young peasant woman had ravished the heart of that mighty king. When that old boy fell for her, he fell *hard.* He was so taken with her that a simple look of love made his knees buckle. The Hebrew word translated *"ravished,"* *livabethini,* has been rendered in almost as many different ways as there are English translations. Some versions translate it as "You have captured my heart," or "captivated my heart," or "charmed my heart," or even "wounded my heart." Each of these renderings is valid because there is no literal interpretation for the verse. However, if we trace *livabethini* back to its Semitic roots, we find that it comes from a word used for tearing bark from a tree. If you tear the bark from a tree, you are wounding that tree and might actually kill it, because the bark is its skin. It protects the phloem layer, which is the equivalent of our circulatory system, bringing the energy produced by the leaves to the rest of the tree. Without the bark, the tree is vulnerable to diseases and pestilences. So God says to us, through this passage, that just once glance of our eye, one expression of love toward Him, causes Him to tear the bark from His heart—to willingly make His heart vulnerable to us.

God voluntarily came to earth to take on human form, where He could suffer physical, emotional, and spiritual pain, and thus understand what we human beings go through when we suffer physical, emotional, and spiritual pain. But from the beginning, He has made Himself vulnerable to heartbreak and the suffering of a wounded heart from the people whom He has created. Just as a wife would be heartbroken if her husband were to sleep with another woman, God would be heartbroken if we were to "go to bed" with another god—if we were to make a god out of wealth, power, status, or anything else that pulled our attention from Him and lessened our devotion to Him.

God knows what it feels like to suffer heartbreak over our unfaithfulness. This is what He was trying to show me. I have proclaimed my love for Him through my blog and my books. He has opened His heart to me, and He has allowed me to enter His heart, to feel His joy and His sorrow, just as a woman would open her heart to her husband so he might share in her joys and sorrows. But like a wayward husband seeking the company of other women and breaking his wife's heart, I have sought other gods, such as status, recognition, and security, and I have broken the heart of the God to whom I have confessed my love.

As I sat before the white tree and looked at the weeping willow tree, I realized that if I were to continue to search for the heart of God, if I wanted to enter those special chambers of His heart, like His weeping room, I had to confess and repent of my infidelity.

41

THE WORLD OF SILENCE

"Whom have I in heaven but You? And besides You,
I desire nothing on earth."
—Psalm 73:25 (NASB)

In his classic, ironic book *The Screwtape Letters*, C. S. Lewis writes about how the senior demon has concocted an effective plan to drive us away from God: he has chosen to sidetrack human beings with noise. He knows that if we are bombarded with countless noisy distractions, we will be unable to hear the voice of God.

Yet the opposite is also true. Being in silence enables us to hear God's voice. Indeed, as my second day of silence—away from noise and distractions—comes to an end, I am beginning to know and recognize God's voice. The world is becoming strangely dimmer, and the supernatural is becoming more natural than the natural. As usual, it took a couple of days to get all the noise out of my head, but I am now entering the world of silence before God and experiencing the delights and sorrows of that world—the delights as God and I speak as if we were old friends sharing our experiences, and the sorrow as I begin to see anew His heartbreak over a lost and dying world.

Oddly, so many things that seemed of prime importance before I left my home in Chicago now appear far less significant, and it seems ridiculous that I fretted over them. I find I am so at peace, having the assurance that God is in control, that I am not at all worried about having to move to a new apartment when I return, or to go back to my bus-driving job, or to deal with many other things that can cause stress in my life. They are so unimportant "in the light of His glory and grace."[11]

This evening, I met with Jesus in the meditation room, and He asked me what I wanted. Again, so many things I might have asked for a few days ago now seem totally inconsequential. Thus, I could think of only two things to ask for, and both were focused on ways to reach people with the message of God's heart.

I have also found that temptations seem almost nonexistent to me here in the silence; to submit to even a mild temptation would seem totally out of place. One reason temptation seems absent is that there is nothing screaming at me to satisfy my personal needs and longings with temporal things. For example, there is no TV distracting me by blaring out the latest product that promises to make my life easier. Additionally, there is no pressure here to be "socially acceptable" and say the right things.

As I experienced during my previous visit here, if you ignore the other people around you, no one feels that is rude, and no one takes offense, because that is what we are supposed to do. There is no talking. However, when I sit across the table from someone during dinner, I still have to get used to this new dynamic. Normally, if you were eating a meal at the same table as someone else, the first thing you would think or feel is, *I must somehow acknowledge this person's presence.* Then you would try to figure out an opening line, such as "Nice weather," or "How's the retreat going so far?" Yet our vow of silence excludes this, so we cannot ask each other any questions; but again, there is no pressure to acknowledge someone and no fear of offending anyone.

I know that such things might seem of little consequence, but I never realized before how they can affect our relationship with the Lord. Maybe it is just me, but social pressure can be a remarkable distraction from God. For example, at church, I am constantly worrying if I greeted someone correctly, or if I said the right words, or if I accidentally offended someone. While I am thinking all this, I am trying to worship God. Likewise, I find it difficult to pray out loud in public. No matter how hard I try to focus on God, I am very aware of those who are listening to my prayer. I wonder,

11. Helen H. Lemmel, "O Soul, Are You Weary and Troubled?" ("Turn Your Eyes Upon Jesus"), 1922.

Did I use the right words? Did I sound "holy" enough? Is my prayer too long or too short?

That is why the Jews wear a tallit when praying or worshipping God. By wearing the prayer shawl, they are essentially saying to the world, "I am shutting myself off from everyone else so I can concentrate on God. I'm sorry if you are offended when I don't acknowledge you, but this tallit signifies I have no social obligations while I am praying and worshipping the Lord." Similarly, in silence, you have no other obligations that might pull your attention away from God. And your prayer can be as long or as short as you want. No one else is listening; no one can make it their business to listen. God alone, in His love and mercy, draws near to listen to you. The psalmist said, *"I love the Lord because he hears my voice and my prayer for mercy. Because he bends down to listen, I will pray as long as I have breath!"* (Psalm 116:1–2 NLT).

42

ATTACHMENT

"My soul, wait in silence for God only, for my hope is from Him."
—Psalm 62:5 (NASB)

The Hebrew word translated *"silence"* in the above verse is *damam*, which means to be still, to be quiet, to be silent, or to be struck dumb. This is another word with a built-in commentary. The first letter is daleth, which denotes a doorway or portal to what is represented by the second letter, mem, which is the revealed knowledge of God, as well as what is signified by the third letter, the final mem, which is the hidden knowledge of God. Thus, silence is a doorway to both the revealed and hidden knowledge of God. I have indeed found this to be true. It is in silence, away from the everyday distractions, that we really do hear God's voice, and He does make known to us the revealed knowledge of His Word, as well as His knowledge that is hidden.

So what do we "wait" for while we are in silence? Actually, the word *"wait"* is not found in the Hebrew text; it was just the opinion of the translator that if you are in silence, you are waiting for something. I am learning that while I am in silence, I am not really waiting for anything, because something is happening all the time. Rather, according to Psalm 62:5, I am *hoping* during this time.

"Hope" is really an unfortunate rendering in this verse for communicating with our twenty-first-century mind-set because, to us, the term has the implication of something uncertain—something that may or may not happen. But the Hebrew word translated *"hope"* comes from the root word

quavah, which means a cord or rope. This is in the sense of a rope that attaches to something. The word *"is"* is also not in the Hebrew text; again, that was the translator's opinion as to what would convey the meaning. If we do a literal, word-for-word translation, what we have is: "Surely does my soul attach itself to God in silence." That doesn't make sense until you have spent some time in silence, and you begin to realize that your soul is attaching itself to God. After two days of silence, my soul is now *quavah*; it is binding with God, or attaching itself to Him.

Our spirit is already attached to God when we accept Jesus as our Savior, but that nasty old body and soul just keep getting in the way. For example, our body wants to eat, so every time we try to fast and praise God, it cries out for food. So we tell it, "Tough luck, kiddo, guess what? I am fasting, and you ain't getting nut'in'." We have to treat it like a spoiled brat, which it is. Believe me, when our body wants something, it will interrupt any important time we have with God, so we just have to tell it to be quiet until we finish getting our spiritual bread from the Word of God.

Then our soul will join in the fray. It may be worried about paying a bill, restoring a relationship, starting a new job, or something else, and those anxious thoughts distract us. Well, we have to just pat our old soul on the head and say, "Now is not the time to worry about it. We are in silence; listen to the voice of God, and He will tell you it is okay."

Quavah, the word translated *"hope,"* has a nautical origin. In earlier days, an anchor was just a big rock with a hole bored through it so a rope could be tied around it. When the rock was tossed overboard into the water, you could be sure that the anchor was still attached to the rope only when you pulled on the rope and felt the stone's weight. You couldn't see the rock that was attached, but you knew from the weight and the fact that your ship was stationary that the rock to which you were anchored was holding firm. As I wrote in part one of *Journey into Silence*, this old ship of my life has been through many storms; the sail is torn and the hull is taking in water. Yet the Rock that I am anchored to still holds.

The next verse continues the nautical theme. Psalm 62:7 in the King James Version says, *"He only is my rock and my salvation: he is my defence [high tower]; I shall not be moved."* High towers were built so sailors could keep the shoreline in view. During a storm, as long as your anchor held and you could see the tower, you could be confident you had not been blown off course. The rock and high tower were a sailor's salvation, and with them, he was confident he had not been moved. When the storm had passed, he would be able to continue on his way.

A funny thing happens to rope when it is put under a strain, such as when it is attached to a rock that is functioning as an anchor. Rope in ancient times was made pretty much the same way rope is made today. Thin strands of fabric are woven together. Each individual strand could easily be broken when strained, but when those individual strands are bound together tightly with other strands, they are greatly strengthened. To really be bound together tightly, the strands have to be stretched. When rope is attached to a rock or an anchor that is lowered into the water, it experiences a pull, and it begins to be stretched. During a storm, a ship is pushed by the waves and wind. But as its anchor holds, the rope that is attached to it pulls the ship back into place, saying, in effect, "You're not going anywhere!" This pull on both ends only tightens the cord or rope. The same is true for us. As we go through the storms of life, our *quavah* is only strengthened. The greater the storm, the stronger our attachment to our Anchor. Our Anchor still holds, and as long as we see the High Tower, or Lighthouse, in the distance, we know we are staying on track to reach our heavenly home.

Yet, as we have seen, it is not only in the storms of life through which our attachment to God, our *quavah*, grows tighter; according to this psalm, it is in silence that our soul grows in its attachment. So again, in silence, I am not waiting for something to happen; it is happening right now. I am binding myself to the Lord. Every moment in silence is making me tighter with God.

43

DANCE TO THE LORD

"Resign thyself unto the Lord, *and wait patiently for Him;*
fret not thyself because of him who prospereth in his way,
because of the man who bringeth wicked devices to pass."
—Psalm 37:7 (JPS Tanakh 1917)

I am studying Psalm 37 as I sit out on the patio watching some birds and a chipmunk at play. During my last visit to the abbey, I learned that if I listen to nature—including birds and animals—closely with my heart, it seems to communicate to me. The chipmunk was looking right at me, as if to say, "Watch this." He then turned and ran up the bird feeder pole to the base of the feeder tray, where three additional birds were helping themselves to seeds. Mr. Chipmunk seemed to be entirely disinterested in the seeds that the bird feeder had to offer; he appeared to be simply at rest beneath the feeder tray, and he stayed there as the birds ate the seeds. Then he looked over at me as if to ask, "Get the message?" Well, actually, I didn't.

After the first three birds at the feeder left, six other birds flew up to the feeder tray, one by one. I counted three black birds, a dove, a cardinal, and one bird that looked like a woodpecker. Including my chipmunk friend, that made seven of God's creatures playing around in front of me. Perhaps this meant I should look at verse seven of Psalm 37; that verse begins, *"Resign thyself unto the* Lord.*"* The Hebrew word translated *"resign"* is *dom*, which comes from the root word *damam*, one of the words I examined yesterday, which denotes to be still, to be quiet, to be silent, or to be struck dumb. I suddenly realized that I did not hear any chirping or singing from the birds; they were just silently going about their business of eating.

There is another meaning for *damam*, which is to stand still, just as Mr. Chipmunk did when he climbed up the bird feeder pole and stood still in front of the feeder tray. He did not partake of any of the seeds; it seemed he climbed that pole for no other reason than the fact that it was there.

Mr. Chipmunk deserved a better title because of the instruction he was providing, so I named him "Pastor Chipmunk." It seemed like he was waiting for something. There he was, surrounded by all that delicious food, but he was having none of it; he was just *waiting*. Then Mrs. Chipmunk joined Pastor Chipmunk, and they ran around in a circle. They stopped, looked at me, and then continued their dance. My heart told me they were communicating something, but I didn't know what it was.

Suddenly, I realized I was reading Psalm 37:7 in English rather than in Hebrew, so I looked in my Hebrew text for the word translated "*wait patiently.*" I found that it is *chul*. I looked at Pastor Chipmunk, who quickly turned around and even seemed to be waving his tail at me, telling me, "You've got it; now let me go about my business."

I checked and rechecked the text, and there was no way around it. For whatever reason, translators had rendered *chul* as "*wait.*" I have no idea how you get *wait* from *chul* because I have never seen it translated that way. *Chul* means to spin around in a circle. I believe this verse would literally read, "Be silent and *dance* for the Lord." But wait, there is more. *Chul* is in a hithpael form, which means it is reflexive; thus, you would render the verse as, "Be silent and *cause yourself* to dance for the Lord." The idea of spinning around in a circle, or whirling, reminds me of how David danced before the Lord in front of the ark of the covenant. The word for "*danced*" in 2 Samuel 6:14 indicates to whirl.

In ancient times, children would worship God by spinning around in a circle. That may be why, when David spun around in a circle before the ark of the covenant, his wife accused him of acting inappropriately for a king; he was essentially acting like a child. David replied, in effect, "Tough, I will act the way I want to act as I rejoice before the Lord." (See 2 Samuel 6:16–22.) David set the example. We must come before the Lord as little children.

"Is that what you are communicating to me, Pastor and Mrs. Chipmunk? That I am to become like a little child in my faith?" Was this a reaffirmation of what God had been telling me? They stopped running in circles and looked at me as if to say, "Well, if you are conversing with chipmunks, you can't get more childish than that."

Hey, there is nothing in the rule book here at the abbey that says I cannot dance; I just need to be silent. Again, the word *chul* is in a hithpael form, meaning I have to cause myself to dance. This will not come naturally to me, so I go back to my cell. I call it my cell, although it is actually my room. However, to me, the room looks and feels much like a prison cell; it has a cold, hard floor; a bed with no springs, just a mattress on a board; a desk—and no heat. It is fifty-five degrees outside, and I believe the temperature is the same in my cell. Well, I did ask for a monk's quarters, not the modern dormitory offered to the retreatants. They reserve about a dozen of the monks' quarters for those who really want to experience monastic life and a contemplative lifestyle. (My recommendation: stay at the retreat house and not the monks' quarters.) Anyway, if anything, my room is private and quiet. If I am going to hithpael, or cause myself, to dance, I must lock my door and shut myself away from the brothers and the other retreatants so no one will think I am crazy.

~

When I went back to my room, I began to *chul*, or to spin around in a circle, worshipping and praising my God. I could not stop because I was experiencing pure joy. If anyone had seen me, they definitely would have thought I was crazy, even here at the monastery. And if they found out a chipmunk had recommended this little dance to me? Well, let's just keep that a secret between you, me, and God.

Don't expect me to get any more rational, because I have vowed to spend the rest of my time in silence practicing the faith of a little child.

44

DELIGHT

"Draw nigh to God, and he will draw nigh to you."
—James 4:8

"Before we search for God, God is searching for us."
—Abraham Heschel

I find the above quote by Abraham Heschel posted all over the abbey. It is interesting that a Catholic monastery would put up a quotation from a Jewish theologian for a Protestant Hebrew teacher to read!

Heschel's quote might seem to be in contradiction to James 4:8. This verse appears to say that if we will search for God, then He will search for us. There is a story in the Talmud that might help to answer this apparent incongruity. I alluded to it earlier when I talked about how Jesus created His own variation on a story from oral tradition when He told His parable of the prodigal son. Here is the essence of the traditional story: A king and his son had a dispute that was so bitter, the son left home and went to live in another kingdom. After some time, the king sent a messenger to his son, saying, "Come home." The son sent the courier back to his father with the reply, "That is too far for me to go." The king sent a second message to his son, saying, "Then come as far as you can, and I will meet you."

The fact is, many people just don't want to be found by God. They say to Him, in effect, "That is too far for me to go." Or they are too busy with their lives here on earth to even be aware of the fact that God is searching for them. But when we begin searching for God, when we draw near to Him, we discover that He has been searching for us all along.

In Deuteronomy 4:29, we learn, *"You will find* [the Lord your God] *if you seek Him with all your heart and with all your soul"* (NKJV). As I search for God's heart during this time of silence, I find I can only go so far; but I have also discovered that if I reach out for Him as far as I can reach, He will meet me. I must, however, take the first steps. I must first want to be found by God.

Notice that in the above verse, it says we must seek Him with all our soul, as well as with all our heart. Our soul is that part of us that expresses our desires. We desire many things, but what place does God have among those desires? To return to the analogy of marriage, a wife will not usually allow herself to be intimate with her husband unless she knows that her husband desires her above any other woman. Similarly, God will not become intimate with us in a spiritual sense unless we desire Him first and have no other gods in our life. To seek closeness with God at the same time we are seeking after other gods puts Him on the level of a mistress or a concubine. The Lord does not want to be our "mistress"; He wants to be the sole God in our life. Only when He knows we desire Him most will He allow Himself to become intimate with us.

How do we desire God more than anything or anyone else? The answer is found in Psalm 37:4: *"Delight yourself also in the LORD, and He shall give you the desires of your heart"* (NKJV). The first step to desiring God, which will lead to intimacy with Him, is to delight yourself in Him. The Hebrew word translated *"delight"* is *'anag*, which means to be delicate and dainty. It comes from a Persian word for being amorous. A woman who is amorous may make a special effort to make herself desirable to her partner. If a wife is going on a special anniversary date with her husband and really wants a romantic evening, she may spend the afternoon getting a facial and going to the beauty parlor, having her hair and nails done. She will wear her best and most flattering dress. In short, she will do everything she can to make herself beautiful for her husband. She will appear to him to be very feminine, a delicate and dainty creature who appeals to the male instinct to protect and shelter. Her behavior declares to him that she is desirous of being intimate with him. Of course, if she goes to all that trouble, and they have an affectionate marriage, he will give her the desire of her heart, which is to be intimate with him.

So how do we become intimate with God? We make ourselves as attractive as we can. We "clean up our act"—ridding ourselves of other gods, putting on the garment of praise, and letting Him know that we want Him, and Him alone. "...*and He shall give you the desires of your heart.*" The Hebrew word translated "*desires*" comes from the root word *sha'al*, a verb that means to inquire or to request. So the word for "*desires*" means a request or a petition—but a request or a petition that expresses a desire. This is not just any request, but a request from the heart.

I journeyed from my home to the abbey to '*anag*, or to make myself beautiful before God so I could *sha'al*, or give Him a request. However, after having gone through this period of cleansing and purging, I find I desire only one thing; I have only one request: just to be intimate with Him. I searched for intimacy with God, only to discover, as Abraham Heschel expressed, that God was already searching for intimacy with me.

45

GREEN PASTURES

"He maketh me to lie down in green pastures."
—Psalm 23:2

I went on a hike today through the woods and pastures, and I was amazed at how green everything was. Afterward, I read Psalm 23:2: *"He maketh me to lie down in green pastures."* The Hebrew word for *"green"* is *deshe'*, which is also a word for grass. There is not much more to say about *"green"* according to our lexicons and Bible dictionaries. But I am curious as to why Scripture says, *"He maketh me to lie down in green pastures"* and not just, "He makes me to lie down in pastures." The word for *"pastures"* is *na'ah*. This term can also be rendered a habitation, a house, or a pleasant place. That should do it: "He makes me to lie down in a pleasant place." So why does it have to be green? I suppose it is important to sheep that pastures be green, because green grass is what they eat. But there may be more to it than that.

I have heard that certain colors seem to promote specific moods in people. There have even been experiments in using color therapy to treat depression and other emotional disorders. Moreover, we often find an emphasis on particular colors in commercial places such as stores. Apparently, red can create excitement, while blue can create a relaxed feel. Green can produce feelings of calmness and tranquility.

I suppose there might be many reasons why the psalmist described the pastures as *"green."* Again, a green pasture would seemingly be plentiful in food and create an atmosphere of peace. Yet, for me, as I walked through the woods and saw all that green, I just had the feeling of *life*.

After contemplating all this, however, I am still unsettled about the meaning of Psalm 23:3. I believe there is something more God wants to teach me about "green," because that seemed to be the purpose of my journey this afternoon. So I decide to see if the word for "*green,*" *deshe'*, has a built-in commentary that can give me a little more understanding about it.

The first letter is daleth, which is a doorway or portal to the next letter, shin, which represents the passionate love of what is signified by the last letter, the aleph, which is God. I feel that God took me through the green pastures to remind me of His passionate love for human beings, demonstrated in His abundant provision for us—from the food we eat to the very air we breathe. (We all learned in elementary school that the green plants, through some chemical interaction with the atmosphere, take in carbon dioxide while releasing oxygen into the air, purifying it.)

It is interesting that the verse says God *makes us* lie down in the green pastures. He has to make us lie down. As I spend this time of silence, I am more aware than ever of how we let the cares of this world dictate our lives. We are so busy, so active, doing things—even things for God—that we never really sit back and enjoy Him. Sure, we have jobs and other responsibilities, and as much as I bask in this week of silence and the simple pleasure of constantly being in the presence of God, I am aware that the week will end and I must return to my everyday activities. But, somehow, we have to learn to set aside times of silence to enjoy the Lord, even in the midst of that busyness.

Furthermore, I am beginning to realize that true retirement from work does not just mean quitting your job and living on social security; it means continuing to find the things that God wants you to do on this earth. Once that is done, you retire to your forever home. I had a friend who was a bachelor and spent his whole life working for an international corporation in their IT department. He helped install their first mainframe and traveled to locations around the world to service their mainframes. It was a good job, an exciting job. And he saved practically every penny he earned. He never purchased a new car or a new home.

He bought used cars and lived in a cheap, one-bedroom house all his life. When he was sixty-two years old, personal computers made mainframe computers obsolete, and he was forced into retirement. He finally had a chance to spend the money he had saved. Except that he was alone, and there was nothing he wanted to spend it on. He had already traveled the world. I did not see him for almost a year after he retired. When I saw him again, I could not believe it was the same person. He was a bent-over, little old man. It was as if he had aged twenty years. Later that year, he died. He didn't have a disease—no heart condition, no cancer, or anything else—he just died. His body simply shut down, because he had no purpose in life.

What my reflections on *"green pastures"* have taught me is that I myself will not be green and filled with life, as in my present state, for too many more years. Most of the green I saw in the woods and pastures today will be gone in a few months, replaced by brown, and that is the state in which I will be when God calls me home. But until that time, I have a mission to fulfill. When I retire from my job, it will not be just to wait to die, as my friend did. I will not leave this planet until my mission is fulfilled. And once it is completed, I can "retire" to heavenly green pastures with my beloved Shepherd, dwelling in His pleasant habitation forever.

46

PRAYER

"And [Jesus] withdrew himself into the wilderness, and prayed.*"*
—Luke 5:16

Apparently, I am in good company when it comes to spending time in silence. Jesus did pretty much the same thing often. In fact, at the beginning of His ministry, He spent forty days in the wilderness fasting. That is when He was severely tempted by the devil but overcame each temptation. Luke's account suggests Satan tempted Jesus *during* the forty days, and Matthew's account suggests that the devil appeared *after* the forty days. No one scholar or church father seems to give an explanation as to why the accounts differ. Generally, it is accepted that Satan tempted Jesus after the forty days, and I will go along with that; I accept that theory because I myself have experienced temptation after fasting. And I have heard many other believers testify that they have suffered assaults from the enemy right after a period of fasting. You may have had a similar experience. I'm not sure why it is that the enemy seems to initiate an attack after we have undergone a time of fasting or living in silence. Perhaps he had already planned the assault, and God called us to fasting and prayer in order to prepare for it. Either way, if God calls us to fasting, prayer, or a period of silence, we had best heed that call. I would hate to come under attack without that preparation of prayer and fasting.

When thinking about Jesus's time in the wilderness, we may wonder, *What did Jesus do for forty days and nights? Was He talking to God the Father the whole time?* That is mostly what I do while living in silence. Which brings us to the question "What is prayer?" That is a good question for anyone who goes into a period of silence. And it was certainly a question that Jesus's disciples wanted to have answered. After they had observed Jesus praying on many occasions, they asked Him, "*Lord, teach us to pray...*" (Luke 11:1). But they added a curious thing in relation to that request: "*... as John also taught his disciples*" (verse 1). Were they asking Jesus to give them the mechanics of prayer, something like, "Bow your head, fold your hands, close your eyes, start with 'Dear Lord,' and end with 'Amen'"?

Jesus answered His disciples by giving them what is known as "the Lord's Prayer," which has been used by many Christians as either a prayer itself or as a model for prayer. For instance, using it as a model, you would start by acknowledging that God is our Father and that He is holy, then pray that His kingdom would be manifested on earth, then ask for our daily needs to be met, and so forth. Unfortunately, my prayers never follow that specific pattern, although perhaps they should. I usually jump right into the "good stuff"—my petitions.

In 1 Thessalonians 5:17, the apostle Paul teaches us to "*pray without ceasing.*" The Greek word for "*pray*" in this verse is *proseuchomai*, which means to exchange wishes or desires, or to interact. The word for "*without ceasing*" is *adialeiptos*, which means just that—unceasing, without an interval. We are to live in a state of continually interacting with God. And that is what I discover to be happening during my time of silence. I am "praying without ceasing."

One of the Hebrew words for "prayer" is *palal*. It denotes intercession, supplication, and making a petition. This term comes from an old Canaanite word for the notched edge of a sword. A sword with a notched edge has been damaged. When a blade strikes something, kinetic energy flows through the blade and into the hand of the sword-bearer. The notch occurs when a strain is placed on the blade as it strikes a blow. A mighty force will cause such a notch in the blade. So the release of kinetic energy, or the setting of energy in motion, creates a physical effect that results in a notch.

There is a similar result, in a spiritual sense, with *palal*, or prayer. Essentially, prayer is releasing our energies toward God to create an effect. However, we don't always direct our energies into prayer the way we should. James 4:2 says, *"Ye have not, because ye ask not."* Additionally, the next verse explains that we do not always receive even when we ask because we ask with the wrong motives. Far too often, we exert our energies in the wrong direction, and our motives are not always pure. For example, I might pray, "Lord give me a candy-apple-red Porsche so I can drive little children to Sunday School," even though an old Ford Focus that still runs well would get them there just as easily. I might pretend my motives are pure, but they really are not: I just want a candy-apple-red Porsche, and the kiddies are just an excuse. Sometimes our impure motives are not quite that obvious, and we need to spend time in fasting and prayer to remove our bad motives and reach our pure motives.

The Talmud teaches that prayer is like a battle between kingdoms. In ancient times, in a physical battle between kingdoms, the winner frequently triumphed by capturing or killing the king. (The same principle applies in certain games, like chess.) Once you overpowered your adversary's king, the war was over; your opponent was defeated. That is why, when a king went to war, he would often dress just like one of his soldiers so the enemy could not spot him or target him. Moreover, the king would be surrounded by his most skilled, brave, and dedicated warriors, and his opponent had to break through those elite guards to reach him. With prayer, this analogy goes only so far, because the "warriors" blocking the way to God are not part of His own army; nevertheless, they are tough soldiers whose only desire is to keep us from reaching Him. Among these warriors are *"the desires of* [our] *flesh"* (Ephesians 2:3) and everyday distractions. That is why we must continually be in an attitude of prayer; this means constantly reaching out to God until we break down all the barriers of the flesh, so that the only motives we have left are pure ones, as well as setting aside all distractions so we can focus on Him.

Jewish men wear a skullcap to remind themselves that they are always in the presence of God, and that everything they do, they do as unto Him. It is to help them remember that they are to continually interact with God, "praying without ceasing." I'm not Jewish, so I do not wear a skullcap. However, I do wear my baseball cap with "Chaim Bentorah Hebrew Teacher" on it for that same purpose (as well as to get the word out about my teaching, of course!).

We can make it our goal to continually be interacting with God—whether during periods of silence or in the midst of our everyday lives.

"And my tongue shall speak of thy righteousness and of thy praise all the day long."   (Psalm 35:28)

"In God we boast all the day long, and praise thy name for ever."   (Psalm 44:8)

47

ROCKS CRY OUT

"And some of the Pharisees called to Him from the crowd, 'Teacher, rebuke Your disciples.' But He answered and said to them, 'I tell you that if these should keep silent, the stones would immediately cry out.'"
—Luke 19:39–40 (NKJV)

"You will find something far greater in the woods than you will find in books. Stones and trees will teach you that which you will never learn from masters [schoolteachers]."
—St. Bernard of Clairvaux

I returned to the great white tree to hear God's lesson for today. As St. Bernard of Clairvaux expressed, stones and trees will teach us things that we could never learn from schoolteachers. When I first arrived at the abbey and looked around the grounds, all I could see were grass, trees, and rocks, along with some birds and squirrels. I wondered where I would get inspiration to meditate on God. Then I remembered the above passage from Luke 19, in which Jesus said that if the people were to stop praising Him, the rocks would cry out in praise. The Greek word translated *"cry out"* is *krazo*, which means an inarticulate shout that expresses deep emotion.

As I sat pondering this great white tree, I wondered just what further lessons I might learn from it. Suddenly, it seemed like the great white tree was crying out with deep emotion, "My roots, examine my roots." I did examine them, and I saw that they went deep into the ground. So deep that, in the many years that the tree has stood guarding the abbey, no storm has been able to blow it down.

I recalled reading in the Talmud that when someone was caught in the fast-flowing waters of a stream, in danger of being dragged under by the rushing water, he would reach for a tree. He would not reach for a branch on the tree, as it could easily break, but he would reach for a root, because that would hold firm.

Yes, another simple lesson from God today. It is one I have heard all my life, so much so that I tend to just overlook it: we must be firmly rooted in the Word of God and in God Himself if we are to stand against the storms of life.

Somehow, thinking about this makes me shiver a little. Is God getting me ready for another storm to come into my life? Is that what my trip to the abbey is meant to be—a preparation? Well, there is one consolation: if God is indeed preparing me for a coming storm, I know it is a storm that He is allowing, and not the result of some stupidity on my part, which has brought about most of the storms in my life.

48

ALL HIS HEART

"And when Delilah saw that he had told her all his heart, she sent and called for the lords of the Philistines, saying, Come up this once, for he hath showed me all his heart. Then the lords of the Philistines came up unto her, and brought money in their hand."
—Judges 16:18

"One sees clearly only with the heart.
Anything essential is invisible to the eyes."
—Antoine de Saint-Exupery[12]

Three times, Samson claimed to have revealed the secret of his strength to Delilah, three times she told the Philistine authorities, and three times they were hoodwinked by Samson. You would think that by the fourth time, they would have gotten wind of the fact that Samson had been playing a little game with them. You know, "Fool me once, shame on you; fool me twice, shame on me." Yet, this fourth time, the Philistines not only went to Delilah, but they also brought money to pay her off. Why were Delilah and the Philistines so certain that this time Samson had really disclosed the truth? The difference is indicated in what Delilah said: "[Samson] *hath showed me all his heart.*"

Expressions from the heart have a significant effect. Have you ever been in a testimony meeting at church? Many churches don't have them

---

12. Antoine de Saint-Exupery, *The Little Prince*, trans. Richard Howard (New York: Mariner Books, 2000), 63.

anymore. Perhaps it is because pastors are worried that someone will start "preaching" and take over the whole service, which is what often happens during a testimony time. And if you try to put a cap on it, someone may say you are "hindering the Spirit." Therefore, if a church does have a testimony time, it usually includes only "popcorn testimonies"—people are allowed to pop up, say a couple of words, and then sit down again. That keeps everyone in line. Besides, testimonies can get somewhat boring when someone unskilled in public speaking doesn't recognize the cues that they are putting people to sleep. However, every once in a while, someone who has no formal training in public speaking will give a testimony that captivates the entire congregation. Everyone is alert and on the edge of their seats, hanging on every word this individual is saying. The reason is that the person is speaking directly from their heart.

The word for "heart" in Hebrew is *lev*, which has numerous meanings, such as thought, reasoning, understanding, will, judgment, design, affection, love, hatred, courage, fear, joy, and sorrow. I have searched for a simple description of the word *lev*, and I believe the best I found was from Rabbi Samson Hirsch, who described the heart as the center of our being, where our emotions are aroused.

In the Western world, we are trained to hide our emotions; this is the reason it is very difficult for many people to share their heart with someone else, or to think with their heart. By "heart," I am not talking about our emotions alone, although our heart is the seat of our emotions. Rather, our heart is who and what we really are.

Someone might tell another person off and then say, "I am not angry about it; I am okay with it. I just wanted you to know how I feel." But that person really *is* angry and has revealed their heart. They may not realize they are angry; they may think they are fine and are just expressing themselves. Others can see their true heart, but they can't. Likewise, a person may say to someone whom they want to correct or reprimand, "I'm telling you this in love." They really believe they are telling that person something in love, but they are actually doing so with resentment or irritation, and they are unable to hide the truth that is in their heart. Sometimes, others can know our heart better than we do. In fact, even animals can know our heart better than we do. A dog can read our facial expressions, hear the tone of our voice, and sense our feelings, recognizing when we are angry, sad, depressed, or happy.

I grew up in a church where I was told not to trust my emotions. That was good advice in general, except I took it too far and did not trust my heart, either. Yet if my heart belongs to God, then it is a significant avenue through which He wants to communicate with me. Thus, during this time of silence, I am letting my heart be my guide. As I mentioned earlier, I am learning to listen to God with my heart, for my heart will hear what my physical ears cannot hear; I am learning to speak to God with my heart, for my heart will speak what my physical lips cannot speak; and I am learning to see God with my heart, for, as the quote at the beginning of this chapter expresses, the heart can see what is invisible to the eyes.

The Talmud teaches that in the spiritual world, there is only one sense. Your spirit does not have a human body that can feel, physical eyes that can see, physical ears that can hear, a physical nose that can smell, or a physical mouth that can taste. Instead, your spirit has the spiritual counterpart of all those abilities wrapped up in one sense. If you can grasp that, and your heart is joined with God's, you will touch, see, hear, smell, and taste things that are too wondrous to describe. Too wondrous because it is all about God, and you will begin to experience how insignificant and, at the same time, how important, you are when you rest in His heart.

49

WHO IS THE KING OF GLORY?

*"Who is this King of glory? The L*ORD* strong and mighty,*
*the L*ORD* mighty in battle."*
—Psalm 24:8

As I experience this time of silence, I believe I am beginning to understand what the glory of God really is. Many people have described the manifestation of God's glory as a cloud or a mist. I heard one pastor say that the glory descended in his church, and it was like a fog. Some have described the glory of God as a heaviness that overcomes them so that they are unable to even stand. The Bible talks about the glory of the Lord filling the tabernacle or temple of Israel such that Moses or the priests could not even enter it. (See Exodus 40:35; 2 Chronicles 7:2.)

Perhaps the glory of the Lord is all those things; I cannot testify to most of them, because they have not been part of my personal experience. It might be that *glory* is an all-purpose word that covers many of the various manifestations of God.

One of the Hebrew words translated *"glory"* in the Bible, such as in Psalm 24:8, is *kabod*. This word is sometimes rendered in English as honor, abundance, riches, splendor, reputation, and reverence. If we trace the word back to its Semitic root, we find that it has the idea of weightiness, heaviness, or a burden. What does heaviness have to do with honor, abundance, riches, splendor, reputation, and reverence? There is one common element—they are all expressions of the love of God.

Love can sometimes feel like a heavy weight and even a burden. In fact, it can become such a burden that it cannot be contained; it has to be expressed. For example, I have heard people who have lost a spouse or who are single by divorce say they wish to be married again because they have so much more love to give. Love wells up inside them, and they want to share it. In fact, love is not love unless it is shared. Many couples find they are so full of love that even sharing that love with each other is not enough to relieve them of that "heaviness," so they have a biological child or spend thousands of dollars to adopt a child in order to have someone else to whom they can express more of the love contained within them.

We all are created in the image of God, and part of that image is not just the ability to love but also the need to love and be loved. Yet we understand so little about genuine love. One of the enemy's main goals is to pervert love, so he tries to confuse us about the nature of love, making it into something merely physical. Our entertainment industry took the phrase "making love," which originally meant to court, or woo, and changed its connotation to that of a one-night stand between a man and woman who barely know each other. The widespread use of that phrase, in that context, shows how much the enemy has succeeded in distorting the concept of love. God created us with the capacity to love; we don't "make" or "manufacture" it, yet the enemy wants us to think about it in that way.

This perspective causes us to turn love inward, so that it becomes something self-centered. For instance, we want to be "in love" because it feels good. Yes, it feels good to receive love, but the devil has warped relationships into something so selfish that if a spouse does not love us enough, we will just leave, get a divorce, and try to find someone else who will love us the way we "deserve" to be loved. Sometimes a person can be so focused on themselves that they will *demand* to be loved in a way that makes them feel right or good; they will even abuse the partner from whom they want to receive love. They might cheat on that person to get their "love" elsewhere, thus "showing" the first partner that they failed to love them the way they feel they should be loved. All of this is a perversion of real love, which originates from God.

We learn in John 3:16 that *"God so loved the world."* Even though much of the world does not return that love, even though people do not love Him back, He still loves. And Jesus taught us to love our enemies; in this way, we will reflect the nature of our heavenly Father. (See, for example, Matthew 5:44.) Our enemies do not love us. But we are commanded to love them anyway.

Earlier, I quoted from Bernard of Clairvaux, one of the founders of the monastic system back in the twelfth century, who was commissioned by the pope to go on a preaching crusade. His weapon was not a sword, like in other crusades, but rather the love of Jesus. His was the most successful of all crusades, but you rarely hear about it. Bernard was so filled with the love of Jesus that it just poured out of him. He could not contain it; again, it was like a burden that had to be lifted, and the only way to lift it was to give it away. He was sent to the Muslim world, to a place of the most radical Muslims of that time, similar to ISIS today. He walked among them as a Christian, knowing his life could be taken at any moment, yet he was so filled with the weight of the love of God that he could not hold it inside. This love was so heavy that it fell upon some of those radical Muslims, and they literally dropped to their knees before God and received Jesus as their Savior. They picked up crosses, and, knowing it would cost them their lives, they paraded down the streets of the radical Muslims, declaring their love for Jesus. For them, too, this love was so heavy, they could not contain it, and it spilled over onto other Muslims, creating a great revival that is even now felt in Muslim communities where there are those who still worship Jesus.

During my time of silence this week, I have felt the love of God overwhelm me. I saw no cloud or fog, nor was I forced to the ground facedown. But I have felt a heavy weight, a weight that made it difficult to even walk; it felt like a cloud of love descending upon me. I did not break out in praise or worship; I simply received that love, because I felt God wanted to give it to me, asking for nothing, not even praise, in return. Could that have been the glory of God? Have I indeed experienced the glory of God at the abbey during my time of silence?

Yesterday, I was so filled with this love of God that I could not keep it inside me. I found a small Wi-Fi hotspot here at the abbey that gave me a few moments of Internet access. I used it to send out to a friend an expression of the love of God that I felt; and when I did, it was like a weight or burden had been lifted, just by sharing a few words about how much I love Him.

So what do we call this weightiness of love, this love that is so heavy in us that we cannot contain it? A love that becomes almost a burden to bear, so that we must find someone or something to whom to pour out that love and relieve us of that burden and weight? I call it *kabod*, or *glory*.

50

THE CLOUD

*"The priests could not stand to minister by reason of the cloud: for the
glory of the* Lord *had filled the house of God."*
—2 Chronicles 5:14

After breakfast on the morning of my fourth day in silence, I noticed
something different among the retreatants. The first day, everyone
came into the dining hall, ate in silence, and left. However, on that morning, people took longer than usual to eat their meals, and when they finished, they did not rush out. Of course, there was nothing to rush to. But
no one was in a hurry to go. They just sat at the tables and stared out the
window as if there was something in that room that kept them there, and
they did not want to leave. Perhaps it was the glory of the Lord. Maybe the
effect wasn't as profound as in the above account from 2 Chronicles, but the
presence of the Lord was there.

One of the ways the Bible describes the presence of God is as a cloud.
The Hebrew word for *"cloud"* in 2 Chronicles 5:14 is *'anan*. In its Semitic
origins, the term comes from a root word meaning an obstacle or a covering. In the Canaanite language, it was used to express the idea of presenting
oneself. It was also used in relation to the practice of soothsaying or to
those who created phenomena; it came from the root word *ayin*, which
means the eye, as in seeing and observing. The word was also used for the
hum of insects or the whispers of leaves. It was associated with soothsayers
because they were known to hum or whisper in their attempts to call up
the spirits.

There is nothing in the word *'anan* that would suggest the moisture or vapors of a cloud. It actually has more of the idea of *seeing a sound*. This "*cloud*" of glory was apparently composed of a sound or vibrations. The Bible says the priests could not stand due to it. As I alluded to previously, I felt something similar yesterday when I tried to take a walk but found it so hard to actually stand and walk that I canceled my hike. I went up to my cell and just lay down on my bunk. Again, I could not even worship or praise God. It was as if God just wanted to love me and not receive anything in return.

There are times when I just want to worship and praise God, but I am not able to, even though I try; yet I feel the presence of God; I feel His love. I wonder how many times, during worship services, we feel that we must *do* something to praise God, or we are not really worshipping. Perhaps God sends the cloud, so to speak, to keep us from praising and worshipping Him so that He can just love us without any expectation of a response from us. True love does not expect anything in return—it only wants to give.

I think I am learning from my time of silence that there are many dynamics to worship. There is worship that involves praise and shouting, and there is worship that is quiet and peaceful. There is worship with uplifted hands, and worship with bended knee or even prostration on the ground before God. There is also worship in silence. During my whole time in silence before God, I have not spoken a word of praise. Yet, I have felt God's love and presence to be just as real and powerful as in any worship service I have ever attended where we were making a lot of noise and telling God how much we love Him.

One of the joys of an affectionate marriage relationship is that each spouse seeks not only to maintain their treasured, shared rituals, but also to discover new and different ways of saying "I love you" to their partner. Even when a husband and wife tell each other "I love you" every day, it can become a duty. Not that saying "I love you" is wrong, but we need to add a little spice to it once in a while, like changing our tone of voice, looking deeply into our spouse's eyes, kissing them on the forehead, or touching their cheek as we say "I love you." In this way, the expression of love will not become routine but will keep its meaning.

One thing I have noticed about many of our churches is that we tend to lock ourselves into one form of worship. When we worship God, we often routinely do the same things over and over again, without incorporating any variety into them. Once more, the danger of doing the same things repeatedly is that they can become a duty rather than a true expression of our heart.

For example, suppose that sometime in the history of a particular church, the Lord moved in a powerful way, and there was an outpouring of the Holy Spirit. Then, after that event, people continued to practice whatever it was they were doing when the Spirit of God fell, hoping to recapture the moment. Thus, if the Holy Spirit manifested Himself while loud music was playing, they continue to play loud music. Another church may practice singing quiet, reverential songs, for that was what was happening when they experienced the presence of God. Still another church may regularly try to reenact the outpouring by jumping up and down, rolling in the aisles, and groaning, because that is how the movement of the Spirit of God manifested on one occasion in their congregation. They repeat these acts as "evidence" of the continued movement of the Holy Spirit in their churches. Yet the Holy Spirit is like the wind or a cloud—you don't know what direction He comes from or where He is going. (See John 3:8.) All you can do is flow with the wind or walk into the cloud and continue in the presence of God.

To further illustrate, suppose I was carrying a set of keys and dropped them on the ground, when suddenly I felt the presence of God—warm, refreshing, and wonderful. I might think, *I have the secret to the presence of God—I just drop my keys!* So the next time I want to experience the presence of God, I drop my keys, but I feel nothing. I think about my first experience and try to imitate just how I held the keys when I dropped them. Was it with two fingers or three? Maybe three would work, because the number three represents the Trinity. I guess not, because there is still no presence. I then consider the height at which I dropped the keys. Was it from waist level or eye level? Maybe eye level would work, because that could represent seeing God. But still I don't feel the presence of God. And so on.

"Ridiculous," you say. Of course, it is ridiculous—about as ridiculous as trying to bring the presence of God by singing a certain song, by playing the electric guitars at a certain volume, by pounding the daylights out of the drums, by singing a quiet, meditative song, or even by living in silence. Instead, we need to continually follow the leading of the Holy Spirit, allowing Him to direct us as we express our love for God and seek His presence.

One last thought: the Hebrew word for "cloud," *'anan*, has another meaning, which is "forbidden." God's cloud is forbidden to all but those who choose to return His love. You see, God loves us and expects nothing in return, but we cannot enter His cloud of love if we do not love Him back. Similarly, a man and woman may love one another, not expecting anything from each other in return. But if the man proposes marriage, giving the woman his heart, and if she gives him her heart, then, oh, how that love will suddenly zoom into ecstasy. However, what if the woman were to reject the man's proposal? His love for her would not suddenly disappear. Rather, it would probably fade over time as he turned his attention elsewhere.

Jesus has proposed marriage to us. He has invited us to live in His Father's house. If we reject this proposal, He will always continue to love us—but we cannot expect to live in His Father's house. Yet if we accept His proposal, and we love Him in return, how His love will soar and be filled with ecstasy! Yes, God loves us with no expectations, but how wonderful for Him (and for us) when we love Him in return.

51

GOD'S HEART

"[Jesus] said, 'Throw your net on the right side of the boat and you will find some.' When they did, they were unable to haul the net in because of the large number of fish."
—John 21:6 (NIV)

It seems my legs are functioning again today. Earlier, I sensed God saying, "Let's go for a walk." The rain had ended, the chill had left the air, and the sun was out. There is a particular trail I walked the last time I stayed at the abbey that leads to a couple of statues, and I decided to follow that trail again. I had not been in the greatest health the first time I walked this path, and the fact that I was able to walk it without having to stop and take a breath is a testimony to God's blessing on my life over these past two years.

After having experienced the overwhelming love and glory of God in such a way that I could barely walk, I figured the ultimate in the joy of the Lord had already passed, but I discovered that was not the case. As I entered the woods, a cloud of love encompassed me, and I felt the Lord saying, "You can praise Me now if you like." I was released to express my love and praise for Him. I could not think of anything I wanted to do more at that moment than to praise and worship Him. It flowed in such a way that I wished it would never end. Then I heard the Lord whisper, "One day it shall never end."

Along the trail, which was surrounded by dense woods, I saw a beam of sunlight pass through the trees and focus on a tall white tree. Here was another white tree! It was as if God was shining a spotlight on it for me. Of course, it just happened to be that time of day when the sun was in the right position to shine through a grove of trees that had a space for a sunbeam. A coincidence, right? After all, there must be many areas where the sun shines through the trees. However, is it just a coincidence that I happened to be there at the right time and in the right spot to see the sun act like a spotlight on the only white tree I have found on this hike—especially when another white tree has become the focus of my attention during my silent retreat? I have learned that when I go into times of silence, there are no coincidences; my spirit is quickened, and I know God is speaking to me.

I noticed a bright red cardinal that seemed to stare at me before flying away to a branch that was in the shape of a heart—if you looked at it from a certain angle, from which I happened to be looking at it. I had told God I was going to be like a little child this week, and therefore this is not a coincidence, either; God is speaking to me.

I am glad my little red friend pointed out the "valentine heart," because the message of the white tree was chilling. I saw that the tree was covered with bark, albeit white bark, so the protective covering was intact. A red cardinal landed on the tree and began squawking away. This time, I recognized the red color as a sign of warning. What was the warning of this white tree with a spotlight on it and a red cardinal chirping away?

And then it hit me. For a long time, I have spoken about *livabethini*, which is the concept of ravishing God's heart, or God tearing the bark off His heart to expose it and make Himself vulnerable to us. However, I never thought that He might close up His heart again. But just as a woman would seal up her heart from her husband if she ever found him seeking the attention of another woman, God will seal up His heart if He ever finds me seeking another god.

For a long time as I walked that trail, I was terrified. I wept out of fear that God would seal up His heart to me. I could not bear the thought that He would close up His heart after He had allowed me to enter it. "Oh, God," I cried, "what must I do so as not to wound Your heart, causing You to seal it up?" I came to a clearing where there was a little lake. Three people, who were obviously locals and not connected to the abbey, were fishing. I looked across the lake and thought, *There are no fish in this lake.*

Just as I thought that, by some strange coincidence, or by "divine incident," one of the fishermen pulled in a beautiful, full-sized fish, which I believe was a trout. I thought of the fact that there are two words in Hebrew for "fish." One is *dag* and the other is *nun*, spelled just like the Hebrew letter. The letter nun represents productivity. It also represents "going with the flow," just as a fish effortlessly rides the currents. Additionally, the nun represents faith. I had no faith that those fishermen would catch any fish, but they did; they believed there would be fish in that lake, and indeed there were.

To have faith is to just go with the flow of God, trusting that He will lead you into productivity. If I flow with Jesus, I will never have to worry about whether or not I am producing enough for Him; He will take care of that. I asked the Lord, "Is that all I have to do in order to keep You from sealing up Your heart?" Instantly, I thought of the verse, "*Without faith it is impossible to please* [God]" (Hebrews 11:6). I can please God by simply having faith and trusting Him. Yes, all I have to do is please Him, and He is the easiest Person to please. If I do, He will never seal up His heart from me.

52

HOLLOWED OUT

*"O Lord God, thou hast begun to show thy servant thy greatness, and
thy mighty hand: for what God is there in heaven or in earth, that can
do according to thy works, and according to thy might?"*
—Deuteronomy 3:24

"Moses was G-d's faithful servant, the greatest of the prophets,
the recipient of the Torah from G-d. Yet after 120 years of the
most G-dly life ever lived, he sees himself as only having begun
in his relationship with G-d!"
—Rabbi Israel Baal Shem Tov

Moses wrote the words in Deuteronomy 3:24 as his life was about to
end. And as I come to the closing day of my time in silence, I find
myself echoing those words: "O Lord God, You have only *begun* to show
Your servant Your greatness." Think about it: had any person witnessed
the power of God more than Moses had? He had watched God save a nation, humble a pharaoh, feed millions of people daily, give the people water
from a rock in the desert, part the waters of a sea to enable the people to
cross over it, and much, much more. I daresay that no one in human history had witnessed the power of God as Moses had; yet after a hundred and
twenty years on earth in which he'd witnessed all those things, he declared
that he had only *begun* to see the greatness of God.

How often do we really think about God's greatness? To gain a glimpse
of that greatness, there are times when we need to just sit and look at a tree,

something I am now doing as I sit on a bench in the courtyard of the abbey, looking at my great white tree, my trysting place with God. We have to really *look* at a tree—each branch, each leaf—and allow ourselves to reflect on what a wonderful work it is. There are millions upon millions of similar trees on this planet, all created by God. Still, they don't even begin to declare a minute part of the greatness of this God who loves us personally and speaks to us personally, as He has done with me this past week.

On the day that he died, the great impressionist painter Pierre-Auguste Renoir sat painting his favorite flower. As he intensely reflected on that flower, his housekeeper, who was bringing his lunch to him, heard him whisper, "I think I am beginning to understand it." Most art historians believe Renoir was referring to the art of painting, but one reflected to me that this was the day he died, and perhaps his mind was on eternal things, and he realized it was God who had given that flower its beauty. Like old Moses, old Renoir was just beginning to understand the greatness of the God whom he would soon stand before.

In Deuteronomy 3:24, the Hebrew word translated *"thou hast begun"* is not what I expected it to be, which was *berith*, meaning beginning. Instead, it is the word *hachiloth*, which is derived from the root word *chalal*. It comes from the idea of wounding, piercing, or weakening. It means to hollow out to form a pipe or to make a flute through which air is blown to make a musical sound. The idea of beginning refers to a beginning that comes from being broken down or hollowed out, so that something beautiful, like music, can flow from us.

Renoir, at the end of his life, realized that to create great beauty, he needed God. Moses, at the end of his life, realized that to really accomplish great things for God, he needed to be hollowed out so that the breath of God could flow through him. Chaim Bentorah, as he sits under this great white tree, suddenly realizes that God has not even begun to hollow him out so that His breath can flow through him to create His beautiful music.

Why, oh why, does it take a lifetime to be hollowed out? And how do we get ourselves hollowed out? Is it by the wounding, the piercing, of our experiences in life? The word *chalal* has a built-in commentary. It is spelled chet, lamed, lamed. The chet signifies a binding with God, and the lamed is a picture of reaching up to heaven to give your heart to God and to receive His heart in return. But wait, there are two lameds. As the ancient rabbis would say, the two lameds represent two uplifted hands in worship, denoting praise and one other thing—surrender. When you surrender to someone, what do you do? You lift your hands to show you have nothing, including no weapons, in them. In your hands and arms lie your power to accomplish things, so by lifting your hands and arms in the air, you are making yourself completely defenseless. You are putting yourself at the mercy of your captor. But in the case of God, you are placing yourself totally at His loving mercy. It is only then that He can begin to do great things through you.

After three score and five years of walking this planet, I am only beginning to understand the greatness of God.

⌒

As I reflect on my life, I cannot help but think of an old song I sang in church as a child:

What have I to dread, what have I to fear,
Leaning on the everlasting arms?
I have blessed peace with my Lord so near,
Leaning on the everlasting arms.[13]

In thinking about this song, I realized that I have not received many hugs in past years. I began to pray, "Lord, I don't want to lean on Your everlasting arms; I want You to hug me with those everlasting arms. Oh, my Lord, I really need a hug right now." Instantly, I felt a warmth envelop me, a peace, and a hug. I heard Him say, "It's okay." You know, everything really is okay. It all is okay when you are resting in that hug, in those everlasting arms. Such peace, oh, such peace, such joy, such rest. I said to myself, *If only this hug would never end.* Then He whispered to me, "One day it shall never end."

---

13. Elisha A. Hoffman, "What a Fellowship, What a Joy Divine" ("Leaning on the Everlasting Arms"), 1887.

53

BESEECH

"And I besought the LORD at that time, saying...."
—Deuteronomy 3:23

In the passage from which the above verse comes, Moses was explaining to Joshua that he had appealed to God to allow him to enter the Promised Land. (See Deuteronomy 3:25.) But the Lord had told Moses that because he demonstrated a lack of faith in front of the Israelites, he was forbidden from entering. God had told Moses to speak to a rock in order to bring forth water for the people. This was the second time the Lord had instructed Moses to bring forth water from a rock, and it came almost forty years after the first time. Formerly, he had been told by God to *strike* the rock with his rod. When he did this, water flowed forth. This time, he was told to *speak* to the rock. Yet he still struck the rock with his rod. (See Numbers 20:7–12.) Nevertheless, water came out.

The Israelites whom Moses was leading knew the story about how Moses had struck the rock with his rod and water had poured out. Now they needed water again, and they were apparently waiting for the "magical" rod to strike the rock. After decades of watching Moses perform miracles with that rod, they had begun to believe there was power in the rod itself. (That might sound ridiculous to us. After all, we know better, don't we? For example, we all know that it is our faith that heals us, not the person who prays for us, such as a healing evangelist. We all know that but, you know, people in those days were not as sophisticated as we are today.)

Anyway, the people were about to enter the Promised Land, and they needed to place their faith fully in God and not in relics. It was time for them to get rid of their misplaced dependence on Moses's rod. Note that God had told Moses to take the rod with him when he spoke to the rock. *"Take the rod, and gather thou the assembly together, thou, and Aaron thy brother, and speak ye unto the rock before their eyes; and it shall give forth his water, and thou shalt bring forth to them water out of the rock: so thou shalt give the congregation and their beasts drink"* (Numbers 20:8). Even though Moses had the rod, he was not to use it as he had forty years earlier; he was only to speak to the rock. Yet when the time came and the people apparently began to pressure him, Moses resorted to the old rod and struck the rock with it.

This is how the Lord responded: *"And the LORD spake unto Moses and Aaron, Because ye believed me not, to sanctify me in the eyes of the children of Israel, therefore ye shall not bring this congregation into the land which I have given them"* (Numbers 20:12). I am not sure where the Sunday school tale came from that Moses was forbidden to enter the Promised Land because he got angry and struck the rock, because it is certainly not biblical. In every translation of the Bible I own, it says that Moses and his brother Aaron, both of whom should have known better, were forbidden to enter the Promised Land because they had not believed God. It seems that Moses had not risen to the level of faith to be able to speak to the rock and bring forth water; he, too, had depended upon the old crutch, his rod, to bring it forth.

Moses knew there was no power in the rod—and yet he didn't know it. Likewise, we know that wearing a cross around our neck has no power, but we allow the enemy to whisper to us, "Wear the cross; maybe it will keep me away, ha ha." Similarly, we hang wooden crosses or pictures of Jesus on our walls, and we lay our Bibles prominently on our coffee tables, while the enemy whispers, "Good job—the Lord will surely bless you now that you have all these relics lying around. Who needs to exercise faith when you've got that cross on your wall and that big Bible in plain sight?" I am not saying that displaying crosses or Bibles is wrong. I appreciate seeing a cross in a church, and I like seeing a cross around someone's neck; I think it is a good conversation starter. Yet when you go too far, as Moses did, thinking that in so doing, you will add a little extra *oomph* to your prayer, then your faith is faltering, and you don't have the faith to enter into the Promised Land.

So Moses was forbidden to enter the land. He blew it; he just didn't have the faith to follow God's instructions. That is scary to me because, if Moses, with his years of seeing the miraculous works of God, still failed, then how much more am I apt to fail? We must always be on guard and never take our faith for granted.

Moses wanted to enter the Promised Land, and he *"besought"* God to allow him to. The word translated *"besought"* is a curious one in Hebrew. It is *'etchanan*, from the root word *chanan*, and it means to be gracious, merciful, and compassionate. Moses was not begging God, as the English word *beseech* would suggest, but he was appealing to God for mercy and compassion. *'Etchanan* is in a hiphal (causative) form, so Moses was caused to appeal to God for mercy and compassion. Sometimes the Lord has to withhold a blessing from us in order to bring us to our knees, to cause us to seek Him, realizing how we have faltered in our faith.

I have spent considerable time here at the abbey thinking about prayer, focusing on the Hebrew word *palal*, which I talked about previously. Yet even with all my reflections on prayer, I fear I will leave the abbey not understanding what prayer really is. Like the disciples, I ask Jesus, *"Teach* [me] *to pray"* (Luke 11:1). I promise myself that I will spend as much time as possible with my Christian friends, grilling them on their knowledge and thoughts about prayer, as well as on their experiences in communicating with God, until they tire of me, and I have gleaned every ounce of knowledge they have on the subject.

I recall reading in the Mishrash Rabbah[14] that prayer is called by ten names: cry, howl, groan, song, encounter, criticism or complaining, prostration, judgment, and—the word for today—beseeching. Prayer is all of these things.

I wrote a book entitled *God's Love for Us* in which I compare our relationship with God to that of a marriage relationship. If you think about the

---

14. A compendium of rabbinic texts that is somewhat like a commentary on the Old Testament.

communication between two people who love each other, you realize that their communication has many different dynamics to it. Sometimes it is quiet, tender communication; sometimes it is criticism or even complaining; sometimes it is singing together; sometimes it is weeping together; and sometimes, as I described previously, it is just lying together, not saying a word but holding each other and enjoying each other's warm presence.

Whatever form it takes, a couple's communication is, in a sense, continuous. For example, when the husband is away from his beloved, his mind remains on her. He is thinking of all the things he will tell her when he returns. When he passes by storefronts and looks at the merchandise, he is contemplating the perfect gift to bring back to his wife to show her how much he loves her. Even though they are separated by a distance, his mind is stayed on her—and that is communication. In this way, he is communicating with his beloved *without ceasing*. You know what? I am enough of a romantic to think that if two people love each other and are separated by a distance, they can both look at the moon at midnight, and, knowing the other person is looking at the same moon, can in some spiritual way feel each other's presence as they share that moon together. If we can be in constant communication with a human beloved in these ways, how much more can we be so with our Divine Beloved?

54

UPRIGHT

"The LORD is righteous, He loves righteousness;
the upright will behold His face."
—Psalm 11:7 (NASB)

What is *"righteousness"*? It sounds important. God loves righteousness, and those who are righteous are able to behold His face. That is everything that matters, in a nutshell—to be what the Lord loves, and to behold His face, or to be in His presence.

"The LORD is righteous." The Hebrew word for *"righteous"* is *tsadiq*, which comes from a root word that means doing what is lawful and correct. The Lord always does what is right; He continually lives by His eternal, spiritual laws. When we receive Jesus as our Savior and are given the gift of the Holy Spirit, God places His eternal laws in our heart. (See Hebrews 8:10; 10:16.) Although as non-Jews, we are not held to the strict Jewish dietary laws or the ritual laws (see, for example, Acts 21:25; 1 Corinthians 8), the apostle Paul made it clear we are still held to the moral laws as listed in the Ten Commandments, and to the laws that God has written on our hearts. Paul emphasized that when we love others as we love ourselves, we will fulfill God's law. (See Romans 13:8–10.) If we follow this way of living, God will love it.

Most believers try to do what is right and follow the moral laws, as well as that which is written by God on their hearts. What the Lord has written on an individual heart may extend beyond what is morally right and wrong to how God has called that particular person to live. For example, the brothers here at the abbey live a disciplined life of silence. They follow the moral law and also their own hearts, which tell them to live a contemplative lifestyle. Not all of us are called to a contemplative lifestyle. We must examine our hearts to determine what lifestyle God has called us to.

Note that three different Hebrew words are used in Psalm 11:7 for the concept of "righteousness," although the first two are related. The first, as we discussed, is *tsadiq*, which is rendered as *"righteous."* The second is *tsedaqoth*, which comes from the same root word and is translated as *"righteousness."* And the third word is *yashar*, which is rendered as *"upright."* The first two words might appear to have the same meaning as the third word; in fact, *yashar* is sometimes rendered in English as *righteous*. However, the Talmud teaches that there are no synonyms in Hebrew, so these words must somehow be distinct.

In its Semitic root, *yashar* means to be straight or level; therefore, it refers to what is right and pleasing to God. *Yashar* is spelled yod, shin, resh. The Talmud teaches that God used the letter hei to create the world and the letter yod to create the world to come. Thus, the yod speaks of the future. In fact, it is the only letter that looks suspended in midair, not extending to the bottom of the line (similar to an apostrophe in English). This letter is often placed in front of a verb to indicate that it is in the future tense. Additionally, even though the yod is the smallest letter in the Hebrew alphabet, it is the first letter in the sacred name of God, YHWH (Yahweh, or Jehovah). Moreover, the yod is viewed as a seed, the smallest grain, which will grow into a big stalk or a mighty tree. The yod represents potential, and hence it is the first letter in the word *yashar*, or *"upright."* We may not be totally righteous now, but we have the seed of righteousness within us, planted by Jesus Christ through His death on the cross, to make us righteous.

The next letter in *yashar* is shin, which is the letter of *esh*, or "fire." With its three uplifted arms, it even resembles a flame. Fire signifies passion and a passionate love for God. It also represents the sun and sun-related words, such as the following: *sh'viv*, "spark"; *shalhaevet*, "flame"; and *sharav*, "heat." Those who are upright have the seed of righteousness planted within them; and their passionate love for God will, like the sunshine, cause that seed to sprout and grow. A passionate love for God will grow in us as we do what is right.

The last letter is resh. The resh is like two perpendicular lines in which the horizontal line is connected at the top of the vertical line, extending fully to the left. This gives the appearance of a single line that is bent over, as if bowing in humility or making a turn. The resh represents repentance and turning away from sin. The upright are those who turn away from wrongdoing. Thus, the *yashar*, or the upright, are those who will experience the presence of God; they are those who have the seed of righteousness implanted within them through the blood of Jesus, and whose seed of righteousness will grow through a passionate love for God. And as the seed grows, it will turn them away from sin. From this, we can see that uprightness is a process, not a state of being.

After having spent almost a full week in silence, I feel discouraged because I am still aware of my sinful self. I am still aware of the many flaws in my life that keep me from being a truly godly man. I think about this as I sit in front of the great white tree, looking closely at it. It is still growing, and it is still producing new leaves every year; it has not yet reached its full potential. And, in the same way, I am still growing and producing "leaves"; I have not yet reached my full spiritual potential.

I have decided that this mighty tree must be an oak because it so strong; it has endured many storms, the loss of its bark, and the ravishes of time, yet it still flourishes. I speak to the mighty tree with my heart, asking, "O great and mighty tree, tree of such awesome strength, just what is it that my God is trying to tell me through you?" The great white tree seems to answer to my heart, "I speak only one thing, and it is this: I was once just a nut like you."

55

HEART OF COMPASSION

"Blessed be God, even the Father of our Lord Jesus Christ,
the Father of mercies, and the God of all comfort; who comforteth us
in all our tribulation, that we may be able to comfort them which are
in any trouble, by the comfort wherewith we ourselves are
comforted of God. For as the sufferings of Christ abound in us,
so our consolation also aboundeth by Christ."
—2 Corinthians 1:3–5

My third journey into silence is almost at an end, and I am enjoying my last meal here at the abbey. As I look around, I notice there are not as many retreatants as there were at the beginning of the week. Perhaps some people never intended to stay more than a day or two. Perhaps they just could not adjust to the silence, or they could not get into this lifestyle. There is a special dining room that the abbey has provided for those who wish to speak with other retreatants during a meal. You are allowed in the room for one meal only. I am pretty much a hermit, so I never desired to speak with the other retreatants. They have their own personal reasons for being here, which are none of my business. However, I have seen more and more people gathering in that dining room as the week has progressed.

On my hike to the statues that I mentioned in chapter 51, "God's Heart," I went back to the little Rosary House Shelter I had visited during my first experience at the abbey. As before, on the walls of this shack were posted prayers, praises, petitions, and other messages from the retreatants' hearts. Some of these notes were folded and tucked into cracks, for only God to read. Others were open for everyone to view. In the open ones,

I learned many reasons why people visit the abbey and spend time in silence—reasons I also summarized in the author's note at the beginning of this book. Some people, like me, simply desire to draw closer to God. Some seek to hear God's voice and receive direction for their lives, some come to work through the grief of a lost loved one, and some desire to find rest and peace in the Lord's presence—but all come to experience God. As I read the many petitions that were posted, I marveled over how there were so many people like me who were just hungry for God and for more of Him. So many who truly loved God.

I noticed that the messages were from people of various backgrounds. Most of the retreatants appeared to be clergy, nuns and priests. You could tell who they were pretty easily just by their bearing and how they handled themselves. But there were others who were obviously not clergy. One guy was over six feet tall and muscular, with the build of a professional football player. He had the steel gaze of one who has gone through some difficult things in life. I would often notice him just sitting outside, looking up at the clouds. Was he praying? Was he reflecting? Why was he here?

While at the Rosary House Shelter, I snapped a photo with my cell phone of the walls covered with all the notes and prayers to keep as a remembrance of the other people who, like me, had come to this abbey with their hearts filled with faith in God and His ability to answer prayer and forgive sins. When I stepped out of the shack, I saw that tall, muscular guy patiently waiting for me to leave. He had his head bowed in prayer. I walked on to the statues, and when I returned, I passed by the Rosary House again. He was still in the shack—on his knees, sobbing.

I do not know what had happened in this man's life, but it was his personal story, and he was here at the abbey in silence, seeking God to soothe his distressed soul. I thanked God that he had chosen to come to the abbey and live in silence in order to deal with his troubled mind, not seeking comfort in drugs or alcohol but in God—in the only way one can find true peace; not a peace that the world gives, but one that Jesus gives, a peace that the world cannot understand. (See John 14:27.)

I recalled a story that an old rabbi related to me when I was a Bible college student and told him I was studying Hebrew. He looked at me and asked why I would want to study Hebrew. I told him that one day I hoped to preach, and I wanted to be able to preach from the depths of the Holy Scriptures. The rabbi nodded knowingly and asked, "So it is to preach that you wish to study the Holy Scriptures in Hebrew?" I said it was something like that. He then told me the story of two men who entered a beautiful tropical rain forest. One was seeking a priceless, ancient relic. The other was seeking the beauty and tranquility of the environment because he had a troubled soul and was seeking rest. Both men returned from their journey having found what they were looking for. The first man found the ancient relic, and he traveled the world, gaining great fame and fortune due to this priceless artifact. The other man found peace and rest for his soul. Many people from all over the world who had troubled souls went to him seeking the secret to his peace. The rabbi then asked me directly, "Are not the Holy Scriptures a beautiful tropical rain forest? And why do you seek to enter it? To find little gems so you can impress your people with your wisdom and knowledge, so they will say, 'Oy, what a learned man you are; come, come, we must sit under your teaching'? Or do you wish to embrace the Holy Scriptures and experience their beauty and peace so that others will come to you seeking the source of your peace?"

I paused to wonder once again why I had come to the abbey to be in silence. Was I seeking some new revelation or experience from God so I could impress my readers with my great knowledge, or was I seeking peace and rest for my troubled soul? I believe it was the latter, and I have indeed found what I was searching for.

I was reminded of my first day on this retreat. I had looked out over the lake, taking in the movement of the small waves and the sparkles of light at the tips of those waves. There were multitudes upon multitudes of sparkles that faded as quickly as they shined. Likewise, I am just one of the multitudes, a flash, an instant, upon this earth, apparently of no more significance than the light next to me or on the other side of the lake. Yet, in my time of silence, I found that despite the billions upon billions of lives whom God has created, I am still special and important to Him. If the physicists are correct, and time is linear, and God lives outside of time, perhaps Jesus has died on the cross billions of times, has suffered and been tortured billions of times, which means He suffered and died for each one of us personally—including me. I could have been one less person for Him to suffer and die for, but He still chose to die for me. Yes, I know that might sound like crazy thinking. You think some strange things like that when you are silent before God. But God's love for us is just as potent and extraordinary as if He had died that many times, suffering for each individual human being personally.

Previously, when I had journeyed to the end of the trail, I found the same two statues I saw the first time I visited the abbey. However, I had remembered the statue of Jesus praying in the garden of Gethsemane looking somewhat different; in my memory, Jesus was kneeling on a rock, praying a polite little prayer. I now saw that He was indeed on His knees, praying, but His head was raised toward heaven in agony, and His hands were covering His face. As I looked at the statue, I felt like He was praying for me personally, as I believe He has also prayed for you personally. He was asking the Father to *"let this cup pass"* (Matthew 26:39) from Him. What was this *"cup"*? Was it the suffering He would experience the next day?

In Aramaic, the word translated *"cup"* in Matthew 26:39 is *casa*, which is also the Aramaic word for a pelican. A pelican has a cup-shaped pouch under its bill, and it was noted for its tender care of its young. If a pelican chick died, it was believed that the mother pelican could resurrect it by feeding it with her blood. I have to wonder if maybe it was not the anticipation of the physical torment to come that caused Jesus to sweat drops of blood in the garden of Gethsemane, but rather His overwhelming love for us, a love like the pelican in the ancient story felt for her chicks, so that she would shed her own blood to free them from death. Perhaps Jesus felt our suffering and agony over our sins so much, and He was so overwhelmed with love for us, that He cried out to the Father to give Him some relief from this all-encompassing grief as He took on our sins. Even while we were yet sinners, Jesus loved us and died for us. (See Romans 5:8.)

Nearby was the second statue, depicting Jesus's disciples asleep in the garden—sleeping while the Savior suffered over their sins. How can we sleep as our Savior agonizes over our sinful state?

I asked myself, *Am I sleeping while my Savior agonizes over a lost world?* I renewed the "deal" with God that I had made on my first visit to the abbey:

if He would weep with me when my heart was broken, I would weep with Him when His heart was broken.

I remembered reading on the Internet about a gunman killing dozens of members of the gay community in Orlando. I read about the gay lovers and partners grieving over their losses. One man cried with a broken heart over the death of his male lover. Despite his loss, I was repulsed over his feelings for his lover, feelings that were not meant to be shared between two men but only between a man and a woman. I couldn't wrap my mind around it, and yet as I later entered the weeping room at the abbey, there was Jesus, holding that man's broken heart and weeping over it. I looked at Jesus and wondered, *How can You weep for someone who has so perverted Your creative design?* But Jesus simply said to me, "He is just a sinner like you, and I love him so. You promised to weep with Me when My heart was broken; will you weep with Me as I weep for this broken heart?"

At first, the whole idea was repugnant to me. Then, all of a sudden, from way down deep inside me—from the very depths of my being, my soul, my heart—I began to weep heavy sobs filled with sorrow, heartbreak, and grief, and I bore the burden of this one whom God loves, standing in the gap for him. I knew and understood that God had once again allowed me to enter the weeping room of His heart and experience His pain.

I recalled the first time after my initial retreat in silence at the abbey when God allowed me to weep with Him over His broken heart. I was driving past a hospital where a Right to Life group was holding a demonstration. The people had signs and banners declaring the rights of the unborn. One sign displayed a gruesome picture of a mutilated fetus that had been aborted. The fight against abortion had never really been my fight. I oppose abortion, but I had never felt much passion for the pro-life movement. I was not even affected by the picture of the mutilated fetus. Hollywood movies had sort of desensitized me to such images. However, I had not driven more than two blocks before I felt a sense of grief, pain, and heartbreak well up in me. It started in the pit of my stomach, and before long, I was weeping uncontrollably. I had to pull to the side of the road as I wept deep, heavy, sorrowful sobs. I knew and recognized that this was not my grief, but that I was feeling God's grief. God was holding me to my part of the deal, and it was my turn to weep for Him over His broken heart—broken over the deaths of millions of lives He created with such anticipation of the joy and pleasure they would bring to Him on earth, lives that had been snuffed out by the enemy.

I thought of that moment, now more than two years in the past but still fresh in my mind and heart. As I concluded my stay at the abbey, my final prayer was that if there were to be any lingering effects of this time of silence, that God would continue to allow me to enter His weeping room. That He would allow me to weep with Him over a lost and dying world. And that maybe, just maybe, He would use me to help bring at least one of those lost souls to Him, so I might wipe at least one tear from my Savior's eye.

EPILOGUE: GOD IS ALWAYS WITH US

"I am with you always, even unto the end of the world."
—Matthew 28:20

I am now sitting on the porch at my home in the suburbs of Chicago. It has been a little more than two years since my first experience of silence at the abbey and about a year since my time of silence in the Catskills. I returned from my third journey into silence just a few days ago, and I am still experiencing new depths into God's heart. The heart of God is infinite, and we will spend eternity exploring it!

Just as I experienced when I returned from my first two silent retreats at the abbey and in the Catskills, a little bird has landed near me on the porch and is looking at me as it chirps and dances. I reflect on my meditations on those two other occasions when I sat on this porch listening to a little bird sing his song to me. I think of the Hebrew word for "bird," *siphar*, and how, in its Semitic root, it is a reference to a bird singing and dancing.

The word *siphar* is spelled sade, pe, resh. The sages used to teach that the sade represents honesty, righteousness, and purity. Indeed, my little feathered friend has a pure heart as he sings his song. Yet if I listen to him with a pure heart of my own, made righteous through the shed blood of Jesus, I may tap into the next letter of his name, pe, which means to speak. I will hear what my friend is trying to say in his little song and dance. As he performs, he is telling me the last letter of his name, which is resh. The resh speaks of the presence of the Holy Spirit.

My new friend has flown here to remind me that even though I am hundreds of miles away from the abbey and the Catskills, the Spirit of God is still with me; He is just as real and present as He was during my silent retreats. Yes, even as I sit here in this noisy, confusing city, the Spirit of God is just as precious to me as He was when I was hidden away in those places of silence.

Once again, I find that I am weeping; however, this time, I am weeping out of pure joy in the presence of Jesus, whom I have learned to love with all my heart.

THE ABBEY OF GETHSEMANI

BEAM OF SUNLIGHT SHINING ON THE WHITE TREE IN THE WOODS AT THE ABBEY

STATUE OF JESUS PRAYING IN THE GARDEN OF GETHSEMANE

STATUE OF JESUS'S DISCIPLES ASLEEP IN THE GARDEN OF GETHSEMANE

EXPLORING THE WORLD OF SILENCE

If you have never spent an extended period of time in silence...

+ What do you think about the following Scripture from Ecclesiastes and Chaim's statement about it?

"Better is a handful of quietness than two hands full of toil and a striving after wind" (Ecclesiastes 4:6 ESV).

"In quietness with God, we produce more than we do with our labors, which can become a consuming passion and a chasing after the wind that will only pass away. What is accomplished in quietness is everlasting; the product of our quietness endures for eternity."

+ Read the following Scripture about silence: *"My soul, wait in silence for God only, for my hope is from Him"* (Psalm 62:5 NASB). Now reread chapter 42, "Attachment."

+ What types of distractions, "noise," or busyness in your life might be preventing you from hearing God's voice more clearly?

+ Begin to incorporate short periods of silence into your life, away from distractions and "noise." For example, you might take fifteen minutes in the early morning just to be quiet before God and listen to Him, take a quiet afternoon walk in a park and talk silently with Jesus, or have a time of solitude right before you go to sleep at night. If personal obligations are preventing you from having time for silence, recruit a friend or relative to help you so that you can make time to be alone with God.

+ Have you ever experienced a *devek*, or a hug, from God, such as Chaim described? Try spending some time just resting in God's presence and allowing Him to love and embrace you as you express your love to Him.

+ Chaim wrote, "All around us, God's creation is continually speaking of Him—do you not hear its calls?" In what ways might God have already used the avenue of creation to speak to you about His beauty, strength, or faithfulness?

+ Make a point soon to spend time in nature to reflect on God's greatness and creativity, and to listen to what He wants to say to you.

+ Explore options for taking an extended silent retreat for a weekend or a full week to give you focused time to seek God without distractions or obligations on your schedule and attention. You might go to a retreat center or rent a cabin in the woods, as Chaim did, or rent a house by the ocean or another location to spend time alone with God.

+ After your period of extended silence, reflect on and answer the questions in the next section.

If you have spent an extended period of time in silence...

+ What was the focus or purpose of your time(s) of silence—for example, drawing closer to God, seeking God's direction and guidance, working through pain or grief, or looking for peace after a difficult experience? What was the overall result of your experience?

+ In what way(s) was being in silence difficult for you?

+ How long did it take to clear your mind of distracting thoughts and other "clutter"?

+ Have you experienced beauty in silence? If so, what was your response to it?

+ Did you hear the world weep, or Jesus weeping for the pain of the world? If so, how did you react?

+ Did God speak to you about something specific in your life? If so, what was it?

+ Did God reveal Himself in His glory, love, or presence in a special way?

+ Did you experience spiritual refreshment or renewed strength?

+ In what way(s) did your relationship with God deepen or change as a result of your time in silence with Him?

+ What passages of Scripture were especially meaningful to you during this time?

+ If you spent time in nature, did the natural world speak to you about God's character, creativity, or purposes? In what ways?

INDEX OF HEBREW, GREEK, AND ARAMAIC TERMS

The following are the meanings of Hebrew letters and words, and Greek and Aramaic words, for primary terms found in *Journey into Silence*. Please see Author's Note at the beginning of this book for an explanation of Hebrew vowel and apostrophe use in this volume.

HEBREW LETTERS

aleph: a unity with God [chapters 39 and 45]

ayin: spiritual insight [chapter 9]

chet: a bridge between two hearts—our heart and God's heart [chapters 11, 15, 20, and 22]; a bonding or binding with God [chapter 15, part three prologue, and chapter 52]

daleth: a doorway or portal [chapter 6, part three prologue, chapters 42 and 45]

gimmel: God's loving-kindness [chapter 2]

hei: God's presence [chapters 6, 20, and 54]; "Here I am" (chapter 26]

kap: a vessel that needs to be filled [chapter 11]

lamed: teaching [chapter 2]; expressing one's heart to God [chapter 39]; reaching up to heaven to give your heart to God and to receive His heart in return [chapter 52]

lamed (double): two uplifted hands in worship, denoting praise and surrender [chapter 52]

mem: the revealed knowledge of God [chapter 42]

mem (final): the hidden knowledge or secrets of God [chapters 11 and 42] nun: the number 50; the fiftieth gate to understanding [chapter 9]; productivity [chapters 15 and 51]; moving through obstacles; "going with the flow"; fish [chapters 26 and 51); faith [chapter 51]

nun (double): a complete understanding; the number 100; completion [chapter 9]

pe: to speak [epilogue]

resh: to move forward [chapter 26]; repentance and turning away from sin [chapter 54]; the presence of the Holy Spirit [epilogue]

sade: honesty, righteousness, and purity [epilogue]

shin: God's passionate love [chapters 2, 20, 39, 45, and 54]; peace and fulfillment found only in God [part three prologue]; fire; spark; flame; heat [chapter 54]

taw: truth and praise leading to repair and restoration [chapter 15]

yod: a message from heaven [chapter 6]; the future; a seed, the smallest grain, which will grow into a big stalk or a mighty tree; potential [chapter 54]

HEBREW WORDS

'ahah: ah; an interjection that expresses helplessness and self-pity [chapter 33]

'alal: diversions; to work; to do deeds; to create a distraction; to be entertained [chapter 36]

'anag: delight; fragile; delicate; dainty; from a Persian word for being amorous [chapters 21 and 44]

'anan: cloud [chapters 9 and 50]; "seeing a sound"; forbidden; in its Semitic origins, comes from a root word meaning an obstacle or a covering; in the Canaanite language, used to express the idea of presenting oneself; also used in relation to the practice of soothsaying or to those who created phenomena, and for the hum of insects or the whispers of leaves [chapter 50]

'anash: desperately wicked; sickly, weak, and frail [chapter 28]

'aqob: deceitful; in its Semitic root, it means a slippery hill [chapter 28] *'arak*: to pant; has the idea of an arousal, a rising of passion or desire; comes from an ancient Persian word meaning to arise [chapter 34]

'atsab: to grieve; a word for intense emotional pain [chapter 40]

'ayil: terebinth; a mighty tree [chapter 4]

baki: to weep [chapter 1]

bara: to create [chapter 10]

baruch hashem: "Blessed be the name" [chapter 31]

batan: belly; womb; in its Semitic root, it refers to the seat of hunger or desire [chapter 32]

chadesh: new things; its root word means to restore or to renew [prologue to part three]

chaeshah chalaqi 'avanim: five smooth stones; the Semitic roots of these words would render the meaning, "an army of hardened hearts mocking" [chapter 24]

chakam: to be wise [chapter 11]

chamesh: five; in the Canaanite language, it denotes an army [chapter 24]

chanak: to train up; in its Semitic root, it has the idea of a "narrowing"; contains the ideas of experiencing something and of being tried [chapter 35]

charad: to tremble; to shake with great emotion [chapter 5]

chashmal: a bright shining object; a shining or gleaming amber or metal; electrum; a compound word meaning "silence" and "speaking" [prologue to part one]

chatam: to seal; to lock up or to stop [chapter 17]

chazah: to behold; from a root word that means to experience [chapter 16]

chul: to wait patiently; to spin around in a circle [chapter 43]

dabar: to speak; signifies words spoken from the heart [chapter 33]

damam: silence; to be still; to be quiet; to be silent; to be struck dumb [chapter 42]; to stand still [chapter 43]

deshe': green; grass [chapter 45]

devek: a clinging to God; a "hugging" of God and letting Him hug you [chapters 13, 19, and 24); to cleave [chapter 19]

dodi: beloved; the idea of two people holding hands [chapter 21]

dom: resign; comes from the root word *damam* [chapter 43]

'etchanan: to beseech; to be gracious, merciful, and compassionate [chapter 53]

hachiloth: to begin; from the root word *chalal*, which has the idea of wounding, piercing, or weakening; also the idea of hollowing out to form a pipe or flute [chapter 52]

halak: to walk (literally or figuratively); a manner of life; in its Semitic root, it has the idea of going or moving, as opposed to just sitting [chapter 25]

halaka: a righteous walk [chapter 25]

harim: hills; a mountain; a range of hills [chapter 26]

'iteka: "with you"; an expression that means, "I am in a relationship with you; I am as near to you as your heart" [chapter 33]

kabod: glory; honor; abundance; riches; splendor; reputation; reverence; in its Semitic root, it has the idea of weightiness, heaviness, or a burden [chapter 49]

kelipos: "a shell"; fleshly thoughts that come during prayer [prologue to part one]

kuwn: to set aright; to prepare [chapter 14]

lev: heart [chapters 1 and 48); thought; reasoning; understanding; will; judgment; design; affection; love; hatred; courage; fear; joy; sorrow [chapter 48]

livabethini: to ravish; to capture; to captivate; to charm; to wound; in its Semitic roots, it comes from a word used for tearing bark from a tree [chapters 40 and 51]

manuchah: rest [chapters 1 and 8); quiet; silent [chapter 1]; still; peace; to give, as in a sacrifice [chapter 8]

na'ah: pasture; habitation; house; pleasant place [chapter 45] *na'ar*: child (male or female); servant; young maiden; three-month-old baby; from an old Persian word meaning to boil; in other Semitic languages, it has the idea of being agitated or stirred up [chapters 33 and 35]

nacham: to repent, with the idea of sorrow and grief more than of turning away from something or of changing [chapter 40]

nachath: quietness [chapter 15]

nahar: stream; river [chapters 26 and 34]

naharot: floods [chapter 26]

n'ameth'a: pleasurable; the pleasure of feasting on a delicacy [chapter 21]

negad: to declare; to tell or speak out in clear, straightforward terms [prologue to part three]

nuchah: peaceful abode; place of quietness [chapter 1]

nun: fish [chapter 51]

'oy: "Where are you?"; a rhetorical, idiomatic Semitic expression that means, "Where are you? You are nowhere" [chapter 25]

palal: prayer; intercession; supplication; making a petition; comes from an old Canaanite word for the notched edge of a sword [chapter 46]

patah: to allure; to deceive; to entice; to persuade; to seduce; its origin carries the idea of simplemindedness, lacking in judgment [chapter 27]

pititani: to deceive [chapter 27]

qadash: to sanctify; to be sacred, hallowed, or held up as something very special [chapter 32]

quavah: a cord or rope that attaches to something [chapter 42]

ra'ah: a consuming passion [chapter 15]

racham: womb; romantic love; tender, caring love; tender mercies [chapter 32]

ranan: to be joyful; to sing; has been used to express a melodious sound or a series of sounds that are in harmony with each other; in its Canaanite roots, the original word was used to describe Bedouins sitting around a campfire at night singing a joyful song without any instruments [chapter 26]

reyqam: void; to be without any effect [chapter 18]

ruach: cool; a spirit; a wind; the mind; an emotion [chapter 25]

saba: satisfied [chapter 16]

satham: inmost (innermost) heart; the "secret place" of the heart [chapter 11]

sha'al: to inquire; to request; the root word for a Hebrew term translated "desires" [chapter 44]

shachah: to worship; signifies spiritual passion and oneness between God and His people [chapter 20]

shalag: snow [chapter 2]

shama': to hear with understanding, attention, and/or a response [chapter 25 and prologue to part three]

sha'on: uproar; a crashing sound, like a wave hitting the rocks on a shore [chapter 1]

shuq: a desperate desire; a desire so powerful you can feel it emanating from someone; a longing or craving; an addiction [chapter 21]

siphar: bird; in its Semitic root, it is a reference to a bird singing and dancing [epilogue]

tearaph: to purge away; to smelt; to refine [chapter 3]

temonah: likeness; to be in someone's image, not physically but in actions and personality [chapter 16]

tsadiq: righteous; comes from a root word that means doing what is lawful and correct [chapter 54]

tsamek: to spring forth; to sprout [prologue to part three]

tsedaqoth: righteousness; comes from the same root word as *tsadiq* [chapter 54]

tov: better; being in harmony with God [chapter 15]

yada: knowing; to know so intimately that you are willing to share your secrets [chapter 23]

yadah: to give thanks [chapter 6 and prologue to part 2]; to confess sins [chapter 6]; in its Semitic origin, it has the idea of shooting an arrow; in its Canaanite origin, it refers to the result of an act [prologue to part 2]

yakach: to reason together; to correct; to bring into right order; to bring into harmony; to be in tune [chapter 2]

yashar: upright; righteous; in its Semitic root, it means to be straight or level [chapter 54]

yatsar: formed; a word used for a potter who fashions a vessel of clay [chapter 32]

yom: day; a twenty-four-hour day; a year; a period of time; a moment of time [chapter 25]

Greek Words

adelphos: brethren, brother [compare with Aramaic *akaya*] [chapter 37]

adialeiptos: without ceasing; unceasing; without an interval [chapter 46]

angelous: angel; messenger [chapter 30]

edakrusen: to weep for others (compare with Greek *klaiontas*) [chapter 38]

elachistos: least; inferior (compare with Aramaic *zeora*) [chapter 37]

klaiontas: to weep for oneself (compare with Greek *edakrusen*) [chapter 38]

krazo: to cry out; an inarticulate shout that expresses deep emotion [chapter 47]

philoxenias: to entertain strangers; to be friendly with strangers; to show hospitality [chapter 30]

proseuchomai: to pray; to exchange wishes or desires; to interact [chapter 46]

ARAMAIC WORDS

akaya: brother, generally used in relation to someone with whom you have gone through a difficult crisis [chapter 37] *casa*: cup; pelican [chapter 55]

madbra: wilderness; a desert; a desolate place; a wild, arid region without inhabitants [chapter 13]

malak: angel; counsel; advice; comes from the same root as the Aramaic words for "king" and "salt" [chapter 30]

roka: spirit, generally used to express the Holy Spirit or the Spirit of God [chapter 13]

sha'al: to ask, out of a real need [chapter 39]

zeora: little, least, or few, in the sense of having little knowledge or ability to work through difficulties or gain understanding [chapter 37]

ENGLISH KEYWORDS AND KEY PHRASES FOR HEBREW, GREEK, AND ARAMAIC TERMS

ah: *'ahah* (Hebrew) [chapter 33]

angel: *angelous* (Greek); *malak* (Aramaic) [chapter 30]

ask: *sha'al* (Aramaic) [chapter 13]

begun: *hachiloth* (Hebrew) [chapter 52]

behold: *chazah* (Hebrew) [chapter 16]

belly: *batan* (Hebrew) [chapter 32]

beloved: *dodi* (Hebrew) [chapter 21]

besought: *'etchanan* (Hebrew) [chapter 53]

better: *tov* (Hebrew) [chapter 15]

bird: *siphar* (Hebrew) [epilogue]

"Blessed be the name": *baruch hashem* (Hebrew) [chapter 31]

brother: *adelphos* (Greek); *akaya* (Aramaic) [chapter 37]

child: *na'ar* (Hebrew) [chapters 33 and 35]

cling: *devek* (Hebrew) [chapters 13, 19, and 24]

cloud: *'anan* (Hebrew) [chapters 9 and 50]

consuming passion: *ra'ah* (Hebrew) [chapter 15]

cool: *ruach* (Hebrew) [chapter 25]

cord: *quavah* (Hebrew) [chapter 42]

create: *bara* (Hebrew) [chapter 10]

cry out: *krazo* (Greek) [chapter 47]

cup: *casa* (Aramaic) [chapter 55]

day: *yom* (Hebrew) [chapter 25]

deceitful: *'aqob* (Hebrew) [chapter 28]

deceive: *patah* (Hebrew) [chapter 27]

deceived: *pititani* (Hebrew) [chapter 27]

declare: *negad* (Hebrew) [prologue to part three]

delight: *anag* (Hebrew) [chapters 21 and 44]

desire: *shuq* (Hebrew) [chapter 21]

desperately wicked: *'anash* (Hebrew) [chapter 28]

diversions: *'alal* (Hebrew) [chapter 36]

entertain strangers: *philoxenias* (Greek) [chapter 30]

five: *chamesh* (Hebrew) [chapter 24]

five smooth stones: *chaeshah chalaqi 'avanim* (Hebrew) [chapter 24]

fish: *nun* (Hebrew) [chapter 51]

fleshly thoughts: *kelipos* (Hebrew) [prologue to part one]

floods: *naharot* (Hebrew) [chapter 26]

formed: *yatsar* (Hebrew) [chapter 32]

give thanks: *yadah* (Hebrew) [chapter 2]

gleam like amber, a: *chashmal* (Hebrew) [prologue to part one]

glory: *kabod* (Hebrew) [chapter 49]

green: *deshe'* (Hebrew) [chapter 45]

grieved: *'atsab* (Hebrew) [chapter 40]

heard: *shama'* (Hebrew) [chapter 25 and prologue to part three] heart: *lev* (Hebrew) [chapters 1 and 48]

hills: *harim* (Hebrew) [chapter 26]

hospitality: *philoxenias* (Greek) [chapter 30]

hug: *devek* (Hebrew) [chapters 13, 19, and 24]

inmost (innermost) heart: *satham* (Hebrew) [chapter 11]

joyful: *ranan* (Hebrew) [chapter 26]

knowing: *yada* (Hebrew) [chapter 23]

least: *elachistos* (Greek); *zeora* (Aramaic) [chapter 37]

likeness: *temonah* (Hebrew) [chapter 16]

new things: *chadesh* (Hebrew) [prologue to part three]

pant: *'arak* (Hebrew) [chapter 34]

pastures: *na'ah* (Hebrew) [chapter 45]

peaceful abode: *nuchah* (Hebrew) [chapter 1]

pelican: *casa* (Aramaic) [chapter 55]

place of quietness: *nuchah* (Hebrew) [chapter 1]

pleasant/pleasurable: *n'ameth'a* (Hebrew) [chapter 21]

pray: *proseuchomai* (Greek) [chapter 46]

prayer: *palal* (Hebrew) [chapter 46]

purge away: *tearaph* (Hebrew) [chapter 3]

quietness: *nachath* (Hebrew) [chapter 15]

ravished: *livabethini* (Hebrew) [chapters 40 and 51]

reason together: *yakach* (Hebrew) [chapter 2]

repented: *nacham* (Hebrew) [chapter 40]

resign: *dom* (Hebrew) [chapter 43]

rest: *manuchah* (Hebrew) [chapters 1 and 8]

request: *sha'al* (Hebrew) [chapter 44]

righteous: *tsadiq* (Hebrew) [chapter 54]

walking: *halak* (Hebrew) [chapter 25]

weep: *baki* (Hebrew) [chapter 1]; *edakrusen* (Greek); *klaiontas* (Greek) [chapter 38]

"Where are you?": *'oy* (Hebrew) [chapter 25]

wilderness: *madbra* (Aramaic) [chapter 13]

wise: *chakam* (Hebrew) [chapter 11]

with thee (you): *'iteka* (Hebrew) [chapter 33]

without ceasing: *adialeiptos* (Greek) [chapter 46]

womb: *racham* (Hebrew) [chapter 32]

worship: *shachah* (Hebrew) [chapter 10]

ABOUT THE AUTHOR

Chaim Bentorah teaches biblical Hebrew, Aramaic, and Greek to lay teachers and pastors in the metro Chicago area through Chaim Bentorah Ministries. He and his study team also conduct regular Sunday services and Bible studies at area nursing homes.

Chaim has a bachelor's degree in Jewish Studies from Moody Bible Institute, a master's degree in Old Testament and Hebrew from Denver Seminary, and a doctorate in Biblical Archaeology. All of his Hebrew professors in college and graduate school were involved in the translation of the *New International Version* of the Bible. In their classes, Chaim learned of the inner workings involved in the translation process. In graduate school, he and another student studied advanced Hebrew under Dr. Earl S. Kalland, who was on the executive committee for the translation work of the *New International*. This committee made the final decisions on the particular renderings used in the original *NIV* translation.

Having done his undergraduate work in Jewish Studies, Chaim was interested in the role of Jewish literature in biblical translation. Professor Kalland encouraged him to seek out an orthodox rabbi and discuss the translation process from a Jewish perspective. From this experience, he discovered many things about the Hebrew language that he had not learned in his years of Hebrew studies in a Christian environment. Later, from his contact with Jewish rabbis and his studies in the Talmud, the Mishnah, and other works of Jewish literature, as well as his studies in the Semitic languages, Chaim began doing Hebrew word studies as devotionals and sending them out by e-mail to former students he had taught during his thirteen years as an instructor in Hebrew and Old Testament at World Harvest Bible College, and those he taught through Chaim Bentorah Ministries.

After self-publishing several books of Hebrew word studies and related topics, Chaim chose ninety word studies to create *Hebrew Word Study: Revealing the Heart of God*, which was his first book with Whitaker House, now followed by *Journey into Silence*. He believes that if we take the time to study the Hebrew language, we can see the true beauty of God's Word and come to know God and His heart in a much deeper way.

Chaim Bentorah Biblical Hebrew Studies
www.chaimbentorah.com
chaimbentorah@gmail.com